RIGHTS VS RESPONSIBILITY
Reconciling our Rights with our Responsibility

BY WILLIAM NITARDY
★ ★ ★ ★ ★ ★ ★ ★ ★ ★ ★ ★ ★

Scripture taken from the New King James Version C 1982 by Thomas Nelson. Used by permission. All rights reserved.

The author has represented warranted full ownership and/or legal rights to publish all the materials in this book.

Rights vs Responsibility
All Rights Reserved.
Copyright C 2017 William Nitardy
V4.0

Cover Design and Internal Page Layout:
Heidi Atwell

Cover Photography:
Black lives matter demo, San Francisco by Jim Killock / Creative Commons; used under CC BY 2.0
Martin Luther King Jr. addresses a crowd from the steps of the Lincoln Memorial where he delivered his famous, "I Have a Dream," speech during the Aug. 28, 1963, march on Washington, D.C. / Public Domain
Declaration Of Independence / © Webking | Dreamstime.com

This book may not be reproduced, transmitted, or stored in whole or in part by any means, including graphic, electronic, or mechanical without express written consent of the publisher except in the case of brief quotations embodied in critical articles and reviews.

ISBN: 978-0-692-90712-2

Printed in the United States of America

Acknowledgements

First I need to acknowledge my wife Diane for putting up with my absence during all those hours that were spent writing this book. Also, her proofreading that identified and corrected many clerical and other errors was invaluable.

Secondly, I want to acknowledge Heidi Atwell who prepared the book for publication, designed the cover and did final edits on the manuscript. She did an incredible job in a very timely and efficient manner.

Finally, I want to acknowledge the many authors and publishers that gave me permission to quote liberally from their works.

Contents

Introduction vii

Chapter 1: Rights 1

Chapter 2: Responsibility...5

Chapter 3: Forms of Racism...9

Chapter 4: Should our Rights be Contingent? 17

Chapter 5: Should a Level Playing Field be Tilted? 19

Chapter 6: Rights and Responsibilities of Ideological Groups 25

Chapter 7: How Should Government Address the Rights and Responsibilities of Ideological Organizations and Groups? 31

Chapter 8: Denying Truth by Inverting Reality.......................41

Chapter 9: How Can Americans be Brought Back to Reality?.............45

Chapter 10: Evidence Explaining the Existence of God and Biblical Truth 49

Chapter 11: Islamic Ideology..59

Chapter 12: Relating Islam to American Anarchy...................65

Chapter 13: Final Thoughts..73

Introduction

People are becoming more and more aware that there is a two-sided ideological war going on in America and around the world with the two sides in diametric opposition to each other. It is basically tearing our country apart on cultural and political issues. The battle is between two diametrically opposite worldviews that have opposite goals, opposite beneficiaries, opposite outcomes, opposite gods and opposite Modus Operandi. I wrote a book titled, "Understanding the Anatomy of Evil" that covers this topic from a broad perspective.

Evidence supporting the existence of this war is everywhere. Kerry Jackson stated:

> In the six weeks since Donald Trump turned politics upside down, we have seen an outpouring of public battiness that has no equal in our history. We thought the lunacy would wear off. But it keeps coming. Politicians, media jesters and celebrities can't stop showing themselves to be completely witless.[1]

Democrats demanded election recounts in battleground states, they blamed James Comey and they blamed Putin. They did everything they could to disrupt the inauguration ceremony. They organized protests and marches all around the country. As usual many of the protests went out of control by attacking police and damaging property. Berkley wouldn't allow a conservative speaker to speak on campus. Normally calm Town Hall meetings shouted down congressional speakers etc.

---

[1] Kerry Jackson, "The Nuttiest Things Democrats Have Said After The Trump Election," http://www.investors.com/politics/commentary/the-nuttiest-things-democrats-have-said-after-the-trump-election/

This book covers a narrow segment of the cultural and political war that was not emphasized in my original book that needs to be disseminated. This segment primarily addresses the rights and responsibilities of groups in America and how the rights of these groups have been elevated through political correctness while their responsibilities have been essentially eliminated. The following article titled "Lawmakers Seek Measures to Protect Citizens from Protester Violence, Intimidation" by Paul Chesser of Liberty Headlines puts this topic in perspective:

> Leftist agitators are escalating their protests into intimidation and violence on campuses in public venues across the country—against elected officials, public figures, and fellow students— and now some lawmakers are saying, "Enough!"
>
> The scale of the liberal resistance ranges from the national to the local. Politico reported yesterday that Republican members of Congress fear violence as they plan to repeal Obamacare. On Inauguration Day former North Carolina Gov. Pat McCrory, while visiting Washington, was forced down an alley and boxed in against locked doors after an intimidating mob stalked him yelling pejoratives, expletives, and threats.
>
> Meanwhile The Daily Caller explained how a loosely connected "resistance" to President Trump has vowed to become "ungovernable," with groups such as DisruptJ20, Black Lives Matter, Refuse Fascism and Occupy Oakland stirring up riots and revolution. And last week Breitbart.com editor Milo Yiannopoulos was prevented from speaking at the University of California at Berkeley due to mob violence.
>
> Even employees of the Environmental Protection Agency joined protests on Monday in Chicago.
>
> So while supporting the demonstrators' rights to free speech, a number of lawmakers around the country have found their behavior to be an infringement on the rights and safety of others, and they intend to sponsor legislation and institute strategies to do something about it.[2]

I have taken the position here and in the original book that since the two sides are polar opposites in every respect, one is as it should

---

[2] Paul Chesser, Liberty Headlines, http://www.libertyheadlines.com/lawmakers-seek-measures-protect-citizens-protester-violence-intimidation/?AID=7236

be and the other is in rebellion against the way things should be and consequently are against what is necessary for a society to be in harmony to allow liberty and justice for all. An overview of the attributes of these opposite worldviews is listed in the table below:

Table of Attributes

Supports The Way Things Should Be	Rebellion against The Way Things Should Be
Believes in God	Rebels against God
Believes in truth	Believes a false narrative
Cares about others	Is self-serving
Believes in equal opportunity	Believes in equal outcome
Respects rights of others	Disrespects rights of others
Believes in negative rights	Believes in positive rights
Supports life for innocent & vulnerable	Rejects life for innocent & vulnerable
Supports capital punishment for guilty	Rejects capital punishment for guilty
Promotes philosophy through rational debate	Promotes philosophy through coercion and ridicule

This book also boldly covers racial groups along with other natural and ideological groups. Now, is an appropriate time to have these conversations on what is wrong with America to promote a better understanding of the real issues and to identify needed solutions.

Chapter 1
Rights

The founding of America was based upon a concept that was very unique. Basically all previous governments were based upon the concept of the Divine Right of Kings where the authority and legitimacy initiated with God, proceeded through the king and then to the subjects. America chose to change that concept since when power was concentrated with the king, he kept the subjects in subjection through tyranny. America chose to have the authority and legitimacy flow from God to the citizens and then to the king or their rulers. This made the leaders the servants and put the citizens in power.

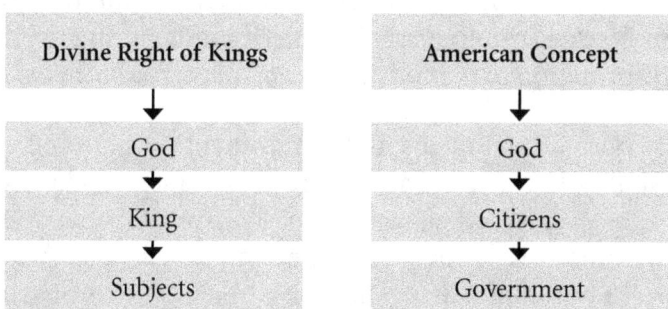

The Declaration of Independence referred to that citizenry as "We the people."

America's birth certificate, The Declaration of Independence, documents our individual, God given rights as citizens. It states that we have the right to life, liberty and the pursuit of happiness. These are all negative rights in the sense that we have a government supporting us against those that would take away our freedom and want to take away our lives, our liberty or wouldn't allow us to pursue happiness. Our subsequent Constitution expanded those negative rights with the Bill of Rights. None of these articulated rights are positive rights that claim that we have a right to government granted money, material goods, special services or some favored status.

Today when we talk about individual rights or group rights it is normally in respect to positive rights bestowed by government that subsidize us or give us special status. America has become like a spoiled child. When it comes to group rights our government identifies special groups that have special rights and a status that are protected from criticism.

President Obama and progressives have identified various "sacred cows" that are above criticism, cannot not be questioned or even objectively discussed. These "sacred cows" include things like homosexuality, abortion, feminism and Islam. However, the most "sacred cow" has to be racism, particularly white on black racism. Racism is the most polarizing and sensitive issue we face as a nation. It is so emotionally charged that any factual information is dismissed as racist. Before supporting the conventional wisdom that extensive white on black racism persists in America and getting overly upset by any information to the contrary read Chapter 3, Forms of Racism.

Typically our culture, media and government do not even consider the possibility that black on white racism is racism. Consequently, when we see overt verbal racism on TV from Obama, Holder or the many other black apologists, they imply it is what we deserve as payback; not angry, arrogant racists that want to promote and establish reverse racism while proclaiming and establishing white on black racism as the most "sacred cow" that cannot be challenged. This is the height of hypocrisy.

I believe that some of the greatest Americans are non-European, non-whites. These include people like Dr. Martin Luther King, Clarence Thomas, Thomas Sowell, Walter Williams, Alan Keys, Allen West etc. These Americans are some of my favorite people. None of them promote the false mantra that it is white racism that keeps blacks as an underclass. If America is so bad for non-European, non-white citizens, why do we have an immigration problem? I am not sure that anybody is against black skin. I don't think that many white people are prejudiced in the sense of the dictionary definition. i.e. an opinion made without adequate basis. However, how do you respect a group that insists on promoting a false narrative that divides our nation?

Rudy Giuliani pointed out the fact that 93% of blacks killed are killed by other blacks. He suggested that the black, roving mobs should address that issue rather than rioting when one of their own bad apples aggressively tries to assault an authority figure and gets killed or badly injured. This is un-American, unethical, unbiblical and totally wrong. The only antidote for a false national narrative is the sunlight of truth!

The objective criticism of the "sacred cow" protected groups is certainly justified and reasonable. Unlike those that support "sacred cow" groups, criticism against those supporters is not coercive. It is only a disagreement or abstaining from approving the protected group.

By establishing "sacred cow" groups, the government not only grants unconstitutional positive rights to some groups, but takes away the natural, negative constitutional rights of other groups at the same time by censoring their free speech or freedom of action. None of these actions are supported by our Constitution. The original concept was, we should not be hindered or be prevented from pursuing life and what we want to do as long as it doesn't interfere with the pursuits of others. It meant that we all have an equal right and an unhindered right to pursue our hopes and dreams. That can be described as equal opportunity. That is not only supported by our Constitution but also by the Bible. Today we seldom hear about equal opportunity.

It is a fair question to ask, "Why does the government create 'sacred cow' groups?" Is it because they care so much for these people in the favored groups? It is hard to know for sure, but in many cases I believe they do care more for these groups of people. We all have favorites. Whether as parents or government leaders, it causes problems when we have favorite children or citizen groups. When we do have favorites, it is best when we make our feelings less obvious and certainly shouldn't publically emphasize or promote our favoritism. In government, your favorites become your natural constituencies. None of that is a problem until the government bestows largess and or special status upon them. What happens is the government and their constituencies partake in a circle of corruption that favors them at the expense of the remainder of citizens. The government bestows largess and special status on them and they vote to keep the government in power so they can continue to exploit the remainder of citizens whether financially or coercing them to accept the group and their beliefs and behavior as legitimate and favored.

More recently, we have rejected the existence of God and have made the government an all-powerful god that can give and take away rights. That not only changed the authority, but changed the standard from the biblical standard of the Ten Commandments and the admonition to "do unto others as we would have others do unto us," to making the government all powerful and the rule-maker. With this godless concept accepted by the masses we either are back to something similar to the "Divine Right of Kings" or something worse, since now we don't even recognize any restraining biblical standards. Now "the ends justify the means" and anything goes to get to where you want to be. Integrity and responsibility are no longer virtues. That is a big problem for freedom going forward and that is why we are attempting to expose the circle of corruption issues between our government and their constituencies in this book.

In the next chapter we will cover responsibility.

Chapter 2
Responsibility

The Oxford Dictionary of current English lists the first three definitions for the word "responsible" as follows:

1. Having an obligation to do something, or having control or care for someone
2. Being the cause of something and so able to be blamed or credited for it
3. Capable of being trusted; reliable

The bible defines responsibility in several texts. One text is the great Commandment found in Matthew 22:36-40:

> [36]"Teacher, which is the great commandment in the law?" [37]Jesus said to him, "'You shall love the LORD your God with all your heart, with all your soul, and with all your mind.' [38]This is the first and great commandment. [39]And the second is like it: 'You shall love your neighbor as yourself.' [40]On these two commandments hang all the Law and the Prophets."

Notice how the first, primary or main commandment concerns our love of God before commanding us to also love our neighbor. I believe that it may be difficult, if not or impossible, to follow the second commandment unless we follow the first.

The second text is known as the Golden Rule and is found in Luke 6:31:

> [31]And just as you want men to do to you, you also do to them likewise.

I believe the best definition our government has ever presented of a citizen's responsibility was part of President John Kennedy's speech where he stated:

> And so, my fellow Americans: ask not what your country can do for you—ask what you can do for your country. My fellow citizens of the world: ask not what America will do for you, but what together we can do for the freedom of man.[3]

Consequently, whether from the dictionary, the bible or from the JFK quote, what is meant by responsibility is clear. Responsibility is something that is directed toward or a duty to others rather than being self-serving. It includes fairness and freedom for all. When we examine ourselves as individuals or as groups that we belong to or a separate group that has an impact on Americans, we need to remember these definitions and use them as the standard to measure against to see if we are being responsible or irresponsible. When we compare groups to this standard it should be using statistical facts and rationale and not based upon emotions. None of these definitions of responsibility included things that you or some group has done in the past. It is all about the current and future situation, so past history shouldn't be part of the discussion, unless it is to learn how to do it better now. Although this applies to both individuals and groups, we are primarily concerned with groups.

We will delineate groups into two types. They are natural groups and ideological groups. We will identify natural groups here and Ideological groups in Chapter 6.

Natural Groups

Natural groups are those that naturally exist where ideology is not the only identification of the group. Political parties and religious organizations are examples of groups that form around ideology and thus are not natural groups. Natural groups include countries, ethnicities, races, etc. Jews with a biological heritage or are from the country of Israel are natural groups, whereas Jews associated with

[3] http://www.presidency.ucsb.edu/ws/index.php?pid=8032&

Judaism as a religion could be considered an ideological group. Even though some people incorrectly consider Arabs and Muslims the same group, Arabs are connected to a biological heritage and thus a natural group whereas Muslims are a religious ideological group.

Here we are primarily concerned with racial relations in America between black Americans and white Americans which we consider natural groups. However, before we address this racism issue, let's consider the country of Israel as a natural group. The following are quotes from "Understanding the Anatomy of Evil," Appendix C and originally came from an article by Bob Barlow.

> Israel and the Jewish people are in the news practically every day. When most people think of Israel, they think of war or religion. However, when one looks at Israel inside, a different picture appears—one of triumph of the human spirit. By the testimony of Israel's own citizens, they have a purpose: **"To find ways of helping other people and nations."** That feeling of responsibility for the world directly contributes to Israel's accomplishments in the economic, technological and humanitarian arenas…
>
> Despite daily challenges ranging from limited resources to security needs, Israeli creativity and inventiveness help make the world a better place. Israel has made significant advancements in the fields of science, environment, medicine and technology, and has willingly and generously shared these developments with the rest of the world…
>
> Why, then, do the nations of the world hate Israel? Ask yourself that question. Don't pass it off as irrelevant. Has Israel benefitted the other countries of the world? Awarding of Nobel Prizes began in 1895 and have since included the areas of physics, chemistry, medicine, economics, literature and peace. Of all the individual awards given since the inception of the Nobel Prize organization, 194 of the recipients have been **Jews**, and they have been recipients in all six award areas. That is 23% of all the Nobel awards ever awarded. As of 2014, eleven Muslims had received Nobel awards, seven of which were for "peace."
>
> Yet, today, Israel is the only nation that has been targeted for removal from the map of the world. Only an illiterate, ignorant, uneducated

person, or a people who are kept in the dark by being told lies about Israel, never allowing them to see their tremendous benefits to their very own nations, would join the voice of "Death to Israel." Those who join that voice will show themselves to be fools, for the God of Israel has stated repeatedly that Israel will be His people forever and ever.

Based upon this information Israel has been a very responsible nation that has made the world a much better place for all of us. In spite of this, Israel is the most reviled nation on the planet. They allow Arabs from neighboring countries to become citizens. They are humanitarian in every respect. The United Nations Human Rights Council has condemned Israel 45 times in resolutions which is about 46% of their total condemnation resolutions. The population of Israel is just over 0.1% of the world and only one country out of 196 countries. Israel probably has the best human rights record of all countries based upon facts. Many of the other countries have horrible human rights records and never get condemned. Many of those countries with horrible human rights records have attacked Israel again and again starting the day after Israel became a nation.

We will examine the racism, animosity and hate between black and white Americans in the next chapter.

Chapter 3
Forms of Racism

The use of the word racism is in some ways similar to the word "love" in English. We only have one word for love in English and it really causes much confusion concerning what we mean when we use that word. The Greek language has four words for love, each with a different meaning. When using Greek, the intended meaning is clear and not confounded like it is in English. In the same way, we use only one word for racism that means many different things and that makes things very confusing. The four Greek meanings for love are as follows:

Agape
This is an unconditional love that sees beyond the outer surface and accepts the recipient for whom he/she is, regardless of their flaws, shortcomings or faults. It's the type of love that everyone strives to have for their fellow human beings. Although you may not like someone, you decide to love them just as a human being. This kind of love is all about sacrifice as well as giving and expecting nothing in return. The translation of the word agape is love in the verb – form: it is the love demonstrated by your behavior towards another person. It is a committed and chosen love.

Phileo
The phileo love refers to an affectionate, warm and tender platonic love. It makes you desire friendship with someone. It's the kind of love which livens up the Agape love. Although you may have an agape love for your enemies, you may not have a phileo love for the same people. The translation of the word phileo is love in the noun – form: it is how you feel about someone. It is a committed and chosen love.

Storge

It is a kind of family and friendship love. This is the love that parents naturally feel for their children; the love that members of the family have for each other; or the love that friends feel for each other. In some cases, this friendship love may turn into a romantic relationship, and the couple in such a relationship becomes best friends. Storge love is unconditional, accepts flaws or faults and ultimately drives you to forgive. It's committed, sacrificial and makes you feel secure, comfortable and safe.

Eros

Eros is a passionate and intense love that arouses romantic feelings; it is the kind that often triggers "high" feelings in a new relationship and makes you say, "I love him/her." It is simply an emotional and sexual love. Although this romantic love is important in the beginning of a new relationship, it may not last unless it moves a notch higher because it focuses more on self instead of the other person. If the person "in love" does not feel good about their relationship anymore, they will stop loving their partner.[4]

Like our word love, racism has many forms and meanings. Let's list and discuss various types of racism beginning with the most severe type.

Hate that dehumanizes and desires destruction

The Nazi's, before taking steps to destroy the Jews and other undesirables, would dehumanize them in their rhetoric. Once we believe that people are not fully human, we will accept anything. The same thing applies to the lynching of black American slaves. We considered black slaves less than human and consequently, anything was permissible. ISIS, and all the various forms of Islamic terrorists groups, behead, crucify, torture, carry-out honor killings and stonings to those that are outside of their religion or not practicing it to their pleasure. Their religion teaches that those outside their religion are included in the house of war (Dar al-Harb) and any war actions against them is justified.

[4] http://thelove.one/four-types-of-love-greek-style/

Just recently Hate Crime charges were filed against four black young people when they taunted, beat and tortured a young, white, mentally challenged man for hours if not days. He was taunted for his disability, his whiteness and his political views. He finally escaped or he might have been killed. Black people are taught today that white people are oppressing them and are the cause of whatever ails them. This isn't much different than the Nazi dehumanization campaign.

Slavery

Slavery is next to the worst kind of racism. It dehumanizes men and exploits their labor and eliminates their negative rights. America has a tainted history of slavery that is certainly shameful and embarrassing. America paid dearly for its sin of slavery with 300,000 dead Union soldiers in the Civil War. Slavery certainly was not uniquely American. It was a worldwide practice. In America it was also not uniquely perpetrated by white people against blacks. There were about 3,500 black slave owners that owned about 10,000 slaves. What is unique is that America fought a war to eliminate slavery. That should be remembered when America is constantly denigrated and never forgiven for their slavery.

Codified discrimination

Even after slavery was ended, laws still existed that discriminated against black people. This is the next most serious form of racism. Segregation laws existed that made them second class citizens regarding use of restaurants, restrooms and other things. Due to the strong leadership of Dr. Martin Luther King, codified discrimination was finally eliminated.

It is worth mentioning that contrary to conventional wisdom, segregation itself was not the evil, it was forced segregation that was evil. I believe that the forced integration that was mandated through bussing etc. was equally evil. Neither segregation or integration is evil in itself, it is the coercion that is evil.

Pejorative speech

Using pejorative speech is the next most serious form of racism. When white people call black people by a derogatory word like the "N" word or when black people call white people "white crackers" that is a big problem. Although the immediate effect of this denigration and disrespect is minimal, unless the underlying attitude can be rectified, this attitude will cause problems going forward. We need to ask a question regarding the legitimacy of the attitude. It is either legitimate or it is not. If it is legitimate, the other natural group needs to make a change and it needs to be made clear how they must change. If not, the source or the unjustified attitude needs to be identified and rectified. Unjustified emotions are normally the problem and trump a rational solution to the real problem.

Not liking the other natural group

In the case of white and black racism, there are two possible causes. The most serious one of these is prejudice resulting by not liking people strictly based upon their skin color. That meets the dictionary definition of prejudice; "an opinion about something or someone that is not based upon reason or experience." The least serious form of prejudice against black or white people is justified negative feelings based upon the other groups' actions and behavior. However, by definition this is not prejudice!

Prejudice without merit

This is true prejudice and although is less serious than all the forms documented above and is not coercive or vindictive in any way it still is disrespectful of the other group and causes bad feelings.

Justified negative feelings

This is the least severe form of negative feelings toward another group. It really shouldn't be called prejudice or bigotry since those negative feelings are justified. Those negative feelings are justified since they are based upon the perceived or real actions of the other group.

Summary

Just like the word "love" is used to mean different things and consequently we can completely misuse the word so sexual lust or exploitation can be confused with caring about somebody. In the same way, racism can be used to label someone with possible justified negative feelings toward another group as if they are the worst kind of racist. This has really been a tool for the black race baiters and apologists to get white people to cower in fear and accept unjustified "white guilt" that forces them to accept any and all demands from blacks.

This confusion is exemplified by a recent internet article titled "Congressional Black Caucus Introduces Bill to Work Toward Reparations" which stated the following:

> Delusional Democrats in the Congressional Black Caucus have reportedly renewed their ill-conceived efforts to force white Americans to pay for the sins of some of their ancestors. Specifically, Michigan Rep. John Conyers and his fellow CBC members have "re-introduced legislation that would set up a commission to consider whether reparations should be paid to black Americans for slavery," according to the Washington Examiner. Conyers has reportedly been proposing the bill every year for at least two decades. As noted by the Examiner, the bill would also consider the prospect of the federal government issuing a formal apology for the "racial and economic discrimination against African-Americans."[5]

I do agree with Conyers that America should formally apologize to black Americans for slavery and for past racism if that hasn't been done in the past. Repentance is always necessary to move forward. However, I do think that there are many things that black Americans should also apologize for including their reverse racism that tries to reverse the playing field rather than level the playing field. These people are not working toward a colorblind society, but are working toward as much black power as they can get.

---

[5] http://conservativetribune.com/congressional-black-caucus-bill/?utm_source=email&utm_medium=C50ConservativeBrief&utm_content=2017-01-05&utm_source=Conservative+50&utm_campaign=5f0430552c-RSS_EMAIL_CAMPAIGN&utm_medium=email&utm_term=0_be457ca6cc-5f0430552c-3350417

A black pastor confirmed the wide spread reverse racism in America as follows:

> There is a race war against white people—a cultural, physical and spiritual war. We saw it very clearly this week in Chicago. Four young blacks kidnapped and tortured a mentally disabled young white man for hours, and they shared video of their cruelty on Facebook Live. They repeatedly shouted, "F— Donald Trump! F— white people!" and made the white victim repeat the same. They forced him to drink toilet water, cut his hair with a knife, even cutting his scalp so it bled, and threatened him physically.
>
> Many pinned this on Black Lives Matter with the hashtag #BLMKidnapping, because it promoted the lie that Donald Trump and white people are "racist"—a lie also pushed by mainstream media, politicians, educators and even preachers. Misled young blacks believe the lie and, due to anger that started in their homes, go into a rage toward white people.
>
> One black woman tweeted, "White people want BLM to be the KKK so they can justify their racism. You don't care about that white boy. You care about being racist."
>
> But Black Lives Matter does not care about that "white boy," nor does it care about Trayvon Martin, Michael Brown or any of its beloved thug "victims." It uses dead black people's names to accuse, hate and usurp power over white people.
>
> The black police superintendent at first claimed authorities had "no concrete evidence" of a so-called "hate crime." Blacks and liberals hated to admit it was a black-on-white "hate crime." Dishonest media falsely presented it as hatred toward people with "special needs," not "white people."
>
> Any honest expert will tell you that blacks are the primary perpetrators of interracial violence (despite so-called "hate crimes" numbers), and that the phony Black Lives Matter movement has no leg to stand on in its false cries of "injustice."
>
> Colin Flaherty's books and YouTube channel document black mob violence, black-on-white crime and hosts of other shocking attacks,

with politicized media cover-up and denial. Heather Mac Donald researches and writes extensively on the Ferguson effect, rising murder rates and "The War on Cops." Jared Taylor's organization published a report, "The Color of Crime," calling out wildly different crime rates among the races. For example, blacks are up to nine times more likely than whites to resist arrest.

The pastor continues:

> I have warned for 26 years that most blacks hate white people—not just black liberals, but many "black conservatives" and black "Christians."
>
> Blacks hate whites because they have no love in their hearts. They don't love their fathers, and they don't know God.
>
> Blacks hate whites because from a young age they're taught a lie that "racism" exists and that only whites are "racist."
>
> Blacks attack, abuse and accuse whites because that's how their mothers and grandmothers treated them. They're only "nice" to you when you agree with them.
>
> Blacks hate because they are angry.
>
> You have no right to be angry. Anger is evil: It spreads and escalates; it causes fear and confusion. Anger is the root of depression and of the wicked Black Lives Matter movement.
>
> Blacks' anger made them the cold, evil, shallow people they imagine whites to be. They identify with "blackness" instead of God, and presume whites guilty until "proven" innocent—and in their darkened minds whites can *never* prove themselves not "racist."
>
> In "The Antidote," I talk about a road rage incident before I overcame my anger. I honked at a white woman who stopped in front of me at a yellow light, and she flipped me off. I got out of my car, cursed and spit on her through her driver window. In my blind anger, I thought *she* was "racist."
>
> For generations, whites failed to tell the honest truth to blacks, fearing blacks' poor reaction, catering to black anger, only making blacks worse. Some young whites face assaults and false accusations

from blacks, and, without a good example from their parents, turn angry. Seeing that anger, blacks in their delusion feel validated passing judgment on whites.

For eight years, Barack Obama escalated the race war, attacking decent white people while pretending violent blacks were innocent victims. He persecuted and reviled good men like Sheriff Joe Arpaio and Donald Trump.

Thankfully, whites and other Americans finally stood up and elected Donald Trump, who exemplifies the good-natured honesty and forcefulness that has all but disappeared in men.

Trump holds no grudges, but he speaks out and fights effectively; he does not back down and does not apologize for being right. He sets a good example that will improve race relations, despite the worst intentions of the Democrats and media.

The evil people opposing Trump, including the media who never questioned Obama but fed hatred and suspicion between the races, show us that we're on the right track in putting down this race war.

More important than restoring sanity in our politics is restoring the moral character of the individual. Toronto professor Jordan B. Peterson, in his New Year's greeting, said that *groups* do not suffer, but the *individual* suffers. Similarly, the individual must deal with his own character flaws.[6]

In the next chapter we attempt to answer the question "Should rights be contingent?"

---

[6] Jesse Lee Peterson, How to End the Race War," http://www.wnd.com/2017/01/how-to-end-the-race-war/

Chapter 4
Should our Rights be Contingent?

Whether our rights are given to us by God or by government, should they be contingent upon anything? I believe the answer is yes. I believe this because of actions God took, what God asked religious and political leaders to do and what God stated in the bible. God stated that we should follow both God's laws and civil laws. In answer to a question regarding whose inscription was on Rome's tax money, Jesus in Matthew 22:21 states:

> And He said to them, "Render therefore to Caesar the things that are Caesar's, and to God the things that are God's."

To show that disobeying God's commandments has severe consequences, God struck down Ananias and Sapphira for lying. God destroyed Sodom and Gomorrah for their sinful living. God ultimately will destroy all people that have not accepted God's redemption plan for us. God asked Joshua to destroy Jericho and many other ungodly peoples. The following text is both a command to Joshua and to all of us (Joshua 1:18).

> [18]"Whoever rebels against your command and does not heed your words, in all that you command him, shall be put to death. Only be strong and of good courage."

I believe that when we disobey the laws of our country or God's Commandments, a temporary or possibly a permanent forfeiture of our rights should be considered even before we have been proven guilty. I believe this is true for both individuals and groups.

One example for individuals is when a robber breaks into someone's home and they are confronted and are either wounded or killed by the homeowner. Many times the peace loving homeowner that is just minding his own business is convicted of a crime against the burglar while the burglar is in the act of a crime. That is a terrible miscarriage of justice when people in the act of a crime continue to have all of their civil rights.

A group example is when we watch the hapless and helpless police do nothing when rioters are looting and burning down property. Again, the criminal thugs are permitted to promote anarchy because while in the act of multiple crimes they retain all of their civil rights. As a minimum we need a law that states that all one's rights are forfeited while in the act of a crime and at least until apprehended by the police. That doesn't mean that police can take drastic action before warning the criminal. Basically all of the people that have been shot and killed by police are resisting arrest and are exhibiting a threat to police rather than following police instructions. Basically all are in rebellion against the police and prefer anarchy rather than a law abiding society.

If the police do something wrong when people are not in rebellion against them and when they are obeying instructions, that is when we need to blame and indict the police. When people are infringing on the rights of others that is when they should lose their rights. It should be thought of in a similar way as the left views economics; a pie that is a fixed size so when the rich people get more that means that the poor people get less. We are not promoting that economic belief here, it is just an analogy. In this case, when someone usurps someone else's rights, that takes away the rights of the other person.

Consequently, if an individual law breaker gets injured or killed as a result of authorities or a third party trying to prevent him from breaking the law or resisting arrest, it is strictly his fault if something bad happens to him. He shouldn't be able to appeal as if he had normal rights.

Whether groups are trying to promote some ideology or just protesting something, we need to consider the need for maintaining a level playing field so rights can be balanced with responsibility. That is the subject of the next chapter.

Chapter 5
Should a Level Playing Field be Tilted?

For each of us there is a great temptation to tilt the playing field in our direction. Whether it is on an individual basis or that of a political party that finds illegitimate ways to stay in power or a group of which we are associated. Rather than follow the "Golden Rule," we often believe that "he who has the gold makes the rules" when we are in the position of power. We are both enamored and consumed with power over others. We can see this when we identify with a dominant sports team that can overpower other teams or in drivers that don't like you to pass them on the freeway. That has been and is the primary evil in our world. We want to be in control so we can tip the playing field in our direction. If we are on the wrong side of the tilted playing field usually we are not content with just having the playing field leveled. We want to reverse the tilt of the playing field so it tips in our direction. If we support having the playing field being reversed we are just as bad as those that tilted the playing field in the first place.

The bible states the following regarding our obligation to be impartial.

> [15]'You shall do no injustice in judgment. You shall not be partial to the poor, nor honor the person of the mighty. In righteousness you shall judge your neighbor (Leviticus 19:15).

> [17]You shall not show partiality in judgment; you shall hear the small as well as the great; you shall not be afraid in any man's presence, for the judgment is God's. The case that is too hard for you, bring to me, and I will hear it' (Deuteronomy 1:17).

> [19]Yet He is not partial to princes, Nor does He regard the rich more than the poor; For they are all the work of His hands (Job 34:19).

[11] For there is no partiality with God (Romans 2:11).

One way political parties stay in power illegitimately is with a circle of corruption. They use money from the treasury (normally supplied by their political opponents) to buy votes from their various constituency groups and promise special treatment to those that donate to their political party.

I believe the clearest example of a past tilted playing field in our country is the racial injustice against black people through slavery. Even when slavery was made illegal the playing field was still not leveled because of forced segregation and unequal rights mandated with laws. It wasn't until Dr. Martin Luther King gave his "I Have a Dream" speech on August 28, 1963 on the steps of the Lincoln Memorial in Washington D.C. that America was willing to pass laws that gave blacks equal legal rights. Even after those nondiscriminatory laws were passed many of us accepted that black people had equal rights but still did not accept them as readily as white people. However, that type of prejudice against people of color has continued to diminish. Today overt white on black racism because of skin color has been greatly reduced. In fact, it is virtually unheard of in any form of speech or text in all media outlets.

However, in many areas reverse racism has emerged with a vengeance. The most obvious evidence of the playing field being tilted the other direction is what we see from our government officials like former President Obama, former Attorneys General Eric Holder and Loretta Lynch. Although virtually no white on black racial speech is heard on media outlets, overt black on white racist speech and text in media outlets and in street speech is rampant. Some of the reverse racism has been coded into law with Affirmative Action and one way hate speech etc. Consequently, the playing field has been tilted in the opposite direction. This is strictly against what Dr. Martin Luther King promoted in his "I Have a Dream" speech. He stated the following:

> But there is something that I must say to my people, who stand on the warm threshold which leads into the palace of justice: In the process of gaining our rightful place, we must not be guilty of

wrongful deeds. Let us not seek to satisfy our thirst for freedom by drinking from the cup of bitterness and hatred. We must forever conduct our struggle on the high plane of dignity and discipline. We must not allow our creative protest to degenerate into physical violence. Again and again, we must rise to the majestic heights of meeting physical force with soul force.

The marvelous new militancy which has engulfed the Negro community must not lead us to a distrust of all white people, for many of our white brothers, as evidenced by their presence here today, have come to realize that their destiny is tied up with our destiny. And they have come to realize that their freedom is inextricably bound to our freedom.[7]

Consequently, the racism in America has reversed instead of just becoming a color blind society. This is completely different than what Dr. King envisioned for black people. The fact that America elected a black president for two terms testifies that white on black racism is not significant in America. However, the fact that in the 2008 election 95% of black people voted for a black president could be construed as a racist vote while the 43% of white people voted for Obama. That shows virtually no racist element in the white vote.

However, many claim that white on black racism is still rampant in America but they don't see reverse black on white racism. One reason for this is that they believe white people still owe black people a huge debt based upon past slavery and discrimination. They believe this debt will exist forever and they have continued animosity toward white people. There is no forgiveness or recognition that attitudes have changed and that the people they resent are different people than those that discriminated against them in the past. It is very unhealthy when we don't forgive people and hold on to animosity according to a book titled "The Bait of Satan." It states the following on the back cover:

> Are you compelled to tell your side of the story?
> Do you fight thoughts of suspicion and distrust?
> Are you constantly rehearsing past hurts?
> Have you lost hope because of what someone did to you?

[7] http://www.americanrhetoric.com/speeches/mlkihaveadream.htm

> *The Bait of Satan* exposes one of the most deceptive snares Satan uses to get believers out of the will of God—offense. This trap restrains countless Christians, severs relationships, and widens the gulfs between us. Jesus said, "It is impossible that no offenses should come" (Luke 17:1). Although you *will* encounter offense, you can choose how you will react.[8]

We are continually reminded of the deficits between black and white on education, income and other areas. One reason for animosity in those areas is that many believe that equal outcome should be expected and any deficit has to be the responsibility of those that are doing better or have more based upon some sort of alleged oppression or prejudice. The belief that the philosophy of equal outcome is justified is not supported in any practical or real context in our world. However, the diametrically opposite philosophy of equal opportunity is legitimate and justified. Belief in either one of these philosophies makes the other philosophy rejected and invalid. Equal opportunity is the philosophy upon which our country was based that made us the greatest country on earth. Equal outcome is basically socialism and has never worked in spite of being implemented over and over again. Justifying equal outcome requires special positive rights laws for special groups that are enforced through government coercion and wealth redistribution. From a biblical standpoint forcing equal outcome violates the commandments against theft and covetousness. Jesus also made a statement that the poor will always be with us (Matthew 26:11).

As you know the bible also teaches that we should have compassion for the poor, orphans and widows. The difference is that the bible teaches that private people and organizations are responsible for helping those in need where true compassion is more than giving them someone else's money. The difference is government coerced vs. private voluntary assistance. The difference is not subtle. One is evil and the other Godly. A book titled "Who Really Cares" by Arthur C. Brooks, documents the fact that it is Republicans, not Democrats, that are the most charitable and among Republicans it is the Christians that are the most charitable even when considering charity over and above what they give to their churches. So much for the conventional

---

[8] John Bevere, "The Bait of Satan," back cover, January 2014.

wisdom that insists that the Democrats are the most compassionate and charitable political group.

With private, voluntary help the recipients typically have some level of responsibility to help themselves. With government handouts the recipients feel no responsibility to help themselves. That gets us back to the title of this book, "Rights vs Responsibility." Individuals are primarily responsible for helping themselves. The government's role is to insure negative rights that prevent others taking away from what is rightfully theirs or ours. When individuals truly need help it is the responsibility of family, friends, churches and the community to help.

With natural groups like the African American community, the Hispanic community, the Jewish community or the white community or other groups etc., the government needs to ensure that their negative rights are not infringed upon. It should not be the government's job to give them positive rights to all kinds of stuff. The latter cannot be done without stealing from others. Besides promoting envy and theft the equal outcome and socialism philosophy destroys the positive relationship between the charitable benefactor and the recipient and the natural corrective action that results. Consequently, the primary economic responsibility for these natural groups needs to be internal to the group. However, private citizens and charitable groups should have compassion where there is a true need.

However, where the need is systemic or generational both the government and the private sector are responsible to identify the root causes and advise the group what needs to be changed to mediate the undesirable situation. This desire to help others should also be used to help other countries as well. A book titled "Poverty of Nations" by Barry Asmus and Wayne Grudem addresses the root causes of poverty in countries and suggests exactly what needs to be done to correct the situation. The same philosophy holds for our country, our cities and our natural groups. The problem is normally a result of lacking integrity. Former congressman, Bob McEwen, identifies the same issues in his DVD titled "Politics: Easy as PIE."[9] Some of the causes are lack of virtuous values, family breakdown, corruption, self-destructive behaviors, lack of incentives, lack of motivation etc.

[9] Bob McEwen, "Politics as Easy as PIE," http://bobmcewen.com/

The idea that people outside of the so-called disadvantaged group are always responsible to dedicate their hard earned resources endlessly to support the same group is neither helpful nor justified.

We need to keep the playing field level and we need to understand that individuals and natural groups are primarily responsibility for their own economic situation. The rest of us can help identify the root cause of the problem and admonish the group to address the root cause. Perhaps even some "seed money" is appropriate when there is good reason to believe it will be used by people with integrity to help the group become self-sustaining. However, what we have done in city after city is to pump in billions of dollars with no expectation of accountability and it has not made the black community any more self-sustaining, but has actually made it more dependent. Detroit went from the richest city on the planet to one of the poorest. Although the actual causes of this downfall are somewhat obvious, it is accepting of the obvious that is the problem. Nobody or any philosophy is ever blamed.

The next chapter will address the rights and responsibility of ideological groups.

Chapter 6
Rights and Responsibilities of Ideological Groups

Almost all groups are ideological groups. They include religious groups, political groups, pseudo-scientific groups, government departments or organizations, humanitarian organizations, charitable organizations and even the natural groups discussed in a previous chapter. By an ideological group we mean groups that have strong beliefs relating to morality and justice within human interactions and activity. Even a singer or music group many times is trying to present an ideological message. Most recently, when a member of the production of Hamilton lectured Vice President Mike Pence after he attended their concert (Hamilton is a musical stage production), they demonstrated an ideological position. The Dixie Chicks demonstrated a similar ideological position when they criticized President Bush. A church choir is normally presenting an ideological message when they are singing. Basically if there is any disagreement on ideas or beliefs it is an ideological issue and when it is promoted by a group it is an ideological group.

Our use of the word "ideology" is intended to be exactly the same as the word "religious." In that context we need to first differentiate between religious and secular and in the religious realm we need to differentiate between true and false religious or ideological beliefs. Virtually all religious and ideological beliefs are two sided positions where the two positions are diametric opposites of each other. Consequently, if one is true the other position is false. Regarding true and false religious beliefs, we first need to discredit the popular concept of relative truth and show that absolute truth does exist. The quote below is from my "Understanding the Anatomy of Evil" book:

> RELATIVE TRUTH
>
> Our postmodern culture has somehow embraced a philosophy of relative truth that denies absolute truth exists…
>
> If one believes in relative truth that means they hold that belief up as an absolute truth. Consequently, those that believe in relative truth believe in absolute truth. If that sounds like an oxymoron, that is because it is. Beyond that, denying absolute truth is unbelievably naive. If someone doesn't believe in gravity, that doesn't mean that gravity is not an absolute truth. The other aspect of relative truth is that it changes truth from something universal and true anyplace and anytime to the idea that truth is just something that an individual believes in. i.e. what is true for you may not be truth for me.
>
> Consequently, with this belief things are only true to the extent that we embrace a specific truth. This contradicts the fact that absolute truths are inherently true. This causes great confusion and this confusion prevents us from recognizing evil and consequently excuses many evils.[10]

Before we can clearly delineate between religious and secular we need to identify the difference between religious beliefs based upon a supernatural God and non-supernatural religious beliefs. We quote again from "Understanding the Anatomy of Evil" as follows:

> DEFINING RELIGIOUS AND SECULAR
>
> The Merriam-Webster dictionary has basically five definitions for "religion." They are:
>
> 1. The service and worship of God or the supernatural
> 2. A commitment or devotion to religious faith or observance
> 3. A personal set or institutionalized system of religious attitudes, beliefs, and practices
> 4. Scrupulous conformity
> 5. A cause, principle, or system of beliefs held to with ardor and faith

---

[10] William Nitardy, "Understanding the Anatomy of Evil," p. 20.

Only the first one is specific about service and worship to a God or the supernatural. The other four basically relate to the secular realm. Let's call these latter beliefs "religious secular" beliefs. I know that sounds like an oxymoron, but that is because we have been programmed to only relate religious beliefs to the supernatural. By doing this the "religious secular" realm can exempt themselves from all the restrictions and condemnation they place on religions that worship a supernatural God...

We need to make one more distinction. The secular realm includes the truly secular realm in addition to the "religious secular" realm. The truly secular realm includes things like your favorite color, sports, homemaking, traveling, hobbies etc. Everyone knows about this truly secular realm. Things in the truly secular realm are never disputed or cause polarization. The problem is that we have been programmed to combine the "religious secular" realm with the normal secular realm in our thinking. The normal secular realm does not cause polarizing debates in culture, politics and religion. By not distinguishing between "religious secular" and purely secular realms the whole atheistic or Secular Humanist religious beliefs or positions get transferred into the secular realm of facts, truth and science rather than being recognized as a religious belief similar to God based religions. At that point they can accuse biblical Christianity of being based upon pure faith and their opposing view being based upon facts, truth and science! Wow, what a scam! Consequently, when we speak of secular issues in this book we are addressing "religious secular" issues.[11]

Again let's quote from my book "Understanding the Anatomy of Evil" as follows:

THE RELIGIOUS REALM

In addition to being programmed not to believe in the two secular realms ("religious secular" and purely secular) we have also been programmed to believe only in one religious realm. This belief is exemplified with expressions like "all roads lead to God" or "all religions are the same" or "good and evil don't exist." Another example is the absence of the words "true" and "false." Religions are all put in the same basket and then denigrated by the bad things

---

[11] William Nitardy, "Understanding the Anatomy of Evil," p. 22-23.

that one or more religions (or possibly specific denominations of a doctrinal religion) have done. We need to look at various religions (doctrinal as opposed to denominational) and compare their beliefs with biblical doctrines and principles and then make a judgment on whether they are good or bad or true or false. This is also true for denominations within doctrinal religions.[12]

The important thing with ideological groups or "secular religious" groups is to withhold your bias and actually objectively study the group's mission or agenda and determine if there is any deceit or lies associated with the ideology they are promoting. Since basically all of the polarizing issues are two diametrically opposite position issues, if one is true the other is false. You can be assured that one position is true and good and the other is false and bad. One side normally is self-serving for a specific group that stretches some liberty into license to benefit a specific group while being a negative factor for others. Just apply the above analysis to the following beliefs or ideological groups and you know where these beliefs or groups fall on the truth or goodness scale:

- Planned Parenthood – self-serving abortion
- Homosexual marriage – not representative of the church's marriage to Jesus or biblical definition of marriage
- Invasion of hordes of Muslim immigrants – they have different values that are incompatible with our Constitution or our traditional values
- Unions – self-serving strikes
- Social justice – equal outcome that violates commandments on theft and covetousness, denies equal opportunity and turns true justice on its head
- Black Lives Matter – self-serving organization to promote black power intended to handcuff cops

Many of these ideological groups stage protests of which many become damaging and dangerous. The next chapter will cover how to deal with those protesting groups by balancing rights with responsibilities. However, let's end this chapter by stating what the bible says about what type of things we should be meditating upon.

---

[12] William Nitardy, "Understanding the Anatomy of Evil," p. 23-24.

The bible states the following in Philippians 4:8:

> **Meditate on These Things**
>
> ⁸Finally, brethren, whatever things are true, whatever things are noble, whatever things are just, whatever things are pure, whatever things are lovely, whatever things are of good report, if there is any virtue and if there is anything praiseworthy—meditate on these things.

It seems as though the things that people are protesting for are the diametric opposite of the things that the bible states we should be meditating on and promoting. The bible endorses and promotes liberty. Some of the texts supporting liberty include Romans 8:21, 2 Corinthians 3:17, Galatians 2:4; 5:1. However, the bible teaches that we need to balance our liberties with responsibilities. Where we go wrong is when we neglect to balance liberty with responsibility, but use liberty as the basis for license.

Chapter 7
How Should Government Address the Rights and Responsibilities of Ideological Organizations and Groups?

When organizations like Christian groups, Tea Party groups or charitable groups etc. gather together to protest, their actions never result in crime, loitering, trashing or any kind of public nuisance. However, when we think of left leaning groups like Occupy Wall Street, Earth Day promoters or even Obama's inauguration supportive attendees or Trump's inauguration protestors, these groups trashed the area wherever they were and required a large police presence. We need to rethink how we view and treat various ideological groups based upon historical evidence and balancing their rights with their responsibilities. We need to require that the leaders and everyone associated with a specific group be held responsible and accountable for all costs including environmental damage, injuries and deaths that group causes when promoting an ideology or a civic protest. Why should someone else always be responsible for costs and problems resulting from a specific group's destructive action?

Congress needs to pass some type of a "Protester Obligations Bill" that would protect their right to protest, but would make them accountable for their actions. In addition, it would ensure that no stealth deceit or misrepresentation would be allowed so their "true colors" would be obvious to all. Beyond protestors, perhaps the bill should require government supported groups like Planned Parenthood to change their name to accurately reflect their true purpose. A more representative title would be Unplanned Unparenthood! We need to somehow expose their pleasant sounding euphemisms that misrepresent their primary mission. This would eliminate unjustified support for their organization based upon their deception.

Although we need to maintain the First Amendment rights for protesting groups and allow them a platform to promote their ideology, I believe a permitting process is needed to ensure that they cannot hide behind any deception and also ensure that any self-serving agenda is exposed and open to public scrutiny during and after that protest.

Perhaps the most important thing is ensuring that ideological groups are legitimate regarding consistency between their true mission and their name or title so we cannot be misled by a name (euphemism) that doesn't represent their true mission. The other requirement that would prevent ideological groups from misrepresenting themselves or deceiving potential supporters would be to have them complete a form that would expose their true mission and their M.O. I believe that the type of protests falls into two categories. One is the promotion of an ideology or agenda. The other is protesting against someone else's policy or law. The following are examples of these two types of completed forms:

Agenda Promotion Questionnaire

What is your organization name or euphemism?

    Black Lives Matter

What are your primary concerns in order of importance?

    1. Blacks killed by cops while resisting arrest

    2. Blacks killed by other blacks (secondary and not promoted)

Is your name or euphemism in sync (agreement) with your main primary concern?

- ☐ Yes
- ☒ No – Our name implies that we are concerned with all black lives, but we are primarily concerned only with black deaths that occur while resisting arrest by cops

Who is your concern for?

- ☐ All Americans
- ☒ Self-serving or a special interest group

Do you have respect for law and order?

- ☐ Yes
- ☒ No

Is one of your goals to gain more power or legitimacy for your group?

- ☒ Yes
- ☐ No

Is your group engaged in "shout downs," censorship or coercion?

- ☒ Yes
- ☐ No

Protesting Concern Questionnaire

What are you objecting to?

    Trump's restrictions on immigration from terrorist countries

What direct effect on America is your primary concern?

    None – Americans would be safer with Trump's restrictions, but that is not what is important to us

Does your concern match the direct primary effect on Americans?

    ☐ Yes

    ☒ No – Our concern is not Americans, it is immigrants

What secondary effects concern you in order of importance?

    1. Inconveniencing travelers

    2. Preventing immigrants from coming to America

Who is your concern for?

    ☐ All Americans

    ☒ Self-serving or a special interest group

Do you have respect for law and order?

    ☐ Yes

    ☒ No

Is one of your goals to gain more power or legitimacy for your group?

    ☒ Yes

    ☐ No

Is your group engaged in "shout downs," censorship or coercion?

    ☒ Yes

    ☐ No

These types of questionnaires would force a designation of whether their concern or what they are promoting is for the benefit of all Americans or whether it may be self-serving or for a special interest group and puts it on display for all to see. They would also make it obvious as to whether the group is concerned about direct effects on all Americans or are more concerned with secondary effects. This would also ensure that their concerns match what they are promoting with their name designation. They must also identify if they support law and order or anarchy. The form will also expose that their real goal is promoting more power or legitimacy for their ideological group if that is the case. Finally, if they practice censorship or coercion, that will be exposed.

For both large and small protests a responsible leader needs be to identified who can and will complete these forms and articulate the group's specific grievances. A large poster of these forms would have to be prominently posted or waved as part of the protest and shown by the media. It should be clear whether they want justice or just legitimacy for their specific cause. The evaluation and approval of these forms should be done in a forum where knowledgeable people, without specific ties to or sympathy for the group, can question them and make sure that their name, mission and actions are consistent and the form is properly completed. Their mission would have to be clear and not a stealth mission hiding behind a better sounding euphemism or the discrepancy would be exposed. The items checked on the forms would have to match their historical behavior.

If the primary grievance or motivation is the desire for more power for their group by usurping the power from other groups, that should be made obvious from the completed form. Power and legitimacy is something that every group and person wants. The question is do they deserve it and is it warranted? To obtain any public support they would need a great story as to why they deserve to get things at the expense of others. One such group that probably deserves more at the expense of others is our veterans. I believe they could demonstrate and get legitimate public support. One would think that the same would be true for our police officers or firefighters. However, currently, the police are being demonized and not supported by our elected officials (before Trump) as documented by Heather Mac Donald in her book titled "The War on Cops: How the New Attack on Law and Order Makes Everyone Less Safe." This is particularly true in urban high crime areas. What we need is to disseminate facts that show how valuable the police really are to us and that when the data is viewed from the correct perspective it shows that cops are not unjustifiably targeting blacks or minorities. Heather Mac Donald is also a very good and articulate speaker. She should be given a megaphone platform to make the facts on this issue eminently clear to our entire country including speaking on college campuses and on all the TV news channels.

Once the form is filled out appropriately and submitted properly, they can get a permit to demonstrate to get attention for their cause. However, they must sign a permit that requires the leaders and every demonstrator be responsible for any problems, criminal actions and cleanup costs. Based upon past experience, perhaps a damage deposit should be required. Perhaps the leader should also be responsible to supply the names and addresses of every participant so justice could be served if needed. Since the demonstrators are giving their support to the group each demonstrator is equally responsible when something bad happens or when costs are incurred.

I am a Tea Party member and I would have no problem agreeing to those terms since the Tea Party is a legitimate organization that only seeks the best for the country and is not self-serving and infringing on the rights of others. If we would protest at a Planned Parenthood facility, the protest would be peaceful, legal and respectful to the environment. I would not fear having to pay for property damage or bodily harm to anybody. The protest wouldn't require any police presence. If counter protesters want to demonstrate, they would also need to have a leader that would take responsibility by getting permitted and identifying all protesters. It may also be prudent to require a delayed protest after the original protest to prevent censorship of the original protester's message and causing unnecessary conflicts. If they caused trouble, they would be responsible for the costs of the police presence and other costs. They would have the full rights of protesting after the protestors they disagree with complete their protest.

Currently, the one group that comes to mind where the above documentation really applies is the "Black Lives Matter" group. That is why we used them on the sample form above. Their euphemism doesn't represent their cause as articulated by their leaders. Their emphasis is only against any police officer that injures or kills a black person no matter what the circumstances or the justification. They have no concern for the magnitudes higher fatalities that result from black on black murder. They have no problem inconveniencing many people by blocking roads or causing other problems. The kind of titles that would actually represent their mission would be something like "Black Power," "Cops: Exempt blacks from enforcement" or "We want to be free to do whatever we want without hindrance or exposure." If they would actually have an honest label they wouldn't get much public sympathy. It is only the deceitful label that gives them a level of legitimacy. Basically, all the evil in our world has to be done by stealth to be supported and thrive. That is why we need to hold groups' feet to the fire to make sure that their cause is legitimate and not allowing them to do evil in the name of doing good by using an unrepresentative euphemistic label.

Before we move on to the next chapter let's briefly discuss the concern or subject of the second example form, Protesting Concern Questionnaire. Immigrants would normally be thought of as a natural group. However, when they differentiate themselves from the natural American group, they become an ideological group. In 1907 Theodore Roosevelt stated the following:

> In the first place, we should insist that if the immigrant who comes here in good faith becomes an American and assimilates himself to us, he shall be treated on an exact equality with everyone else, for it is an outrage to discriminate against any such man because of creed, or birthplace, or origin. But this is predicated upon the person becoming in every facet American, and nothing but an American … There can be no divided allegiance here. Any man that says he is an American, but something else also, isn't an American at all. We have

room for but one flag, the American flag … We have room for but one language here, and that is the English language … and we have room for but one sole loyalty to the American people.[13]

I believe that his comments are appropriate for Muslim immigrants specifically for several reasons.

1. They come here as a group of refugees from a common location with the same religion, political beliefs and customs.
2. Muslims are known for lack of integration whether within the US or in Europe.
3. Discovered documents from Islamic organizations and leaders indicate that immigration is their method of stealth Jihad.

The following letter to the editor supports the number 3 item above:

Should America defend Islam?

The following excerpt is from an official document presented as evidence at the "Holyland Foundation Trial" which outlines the Muslim Brotherhood's strategic goals for North America.

> "The process of settlement is a 'Civilization-Jihadist Process'… The Ikhwan [Muslim Brotherhood] must understand that their work in America is a kind of grand jihad in eliminating and destroying the Western civilization from within and 'sabotaging' its miserable house by their hands and the hands of the believers…"

Khalid Sheikh Mohammed, the 911 mastermind, said the following:

> "The 'practical' way to defeat America was through immigration and by outbreeding non-Muslims." He said "jihadi-minded brothers would immigrate into the United States, taking advantage of the welfare system to support themselves while they spread their jihadi message. They will wrap themselves in America's rights and laws for protection, ratchet up acceptance of Sharia law, and then, only when they were strong enough, rise up and violently impose Sharia from within."

[13] Snopes.com

President Donald Trump understands that Islam is a totalitarian ideology that wants to destroy America and is attempting to halt the suicidal immigration of refugees from countries where terror is prevalent to protect America. However, politically correct, multicultural apologists demonstrate against Trump and insist on an uninhibited flow of Muslim immigrants.[14]

Next we want to address how individuals and groups deny truth by inverting reality.

---

[14] Bill Nitardy, 1/30/2017.

Chapter 8
Denying Truth by Inverting Reality

The relationship between a real image (reality) and the image on a photographic negative in a camera is a perfect analogy describing the difference between the real world of facts and truth and the false cultural, political and religious images being promoted in America and around the world today. An actual image is the embodiment of truth and reality whereas the image produced on a photographic film in a camera is the opposite in every respect. The right side of the actual image is transposed to the left side on the film negative and the top of the actual image is transposed to the bottom on the film negative and vice versa. That is not all that has been inverted. The brightest sources of light on the actual image are transposed to be the darkest part on the negative of the image and vice versa.

It is possible and actually likely that you may not relate this concept to anything in the cultural, political and religious realm. However, some of the categorical areas where this concept would apply are as follows:

1. Political Correctness – Cultural Marxism – Diametrically opposed to biblical principles
2. The New Tolerance – Censor dialogue and demonize the messenger – Coined by Josh McDowell
3. Outrage Based Coerced Conscience – Forcing people to condone beliefs and lifestyles – Coined by Bill Nitardy
4. Euphemisms – A woman's right to choose, Black lives matter, Planned Parenthood etc.
5. Negative labeling – Racist, Homophobe, Xenophobe, Deplorables, etc.

6. False religions – Secular Humanism, Islam, New Age etc. – Diametric opposites to biblical Christianity

Some additional, more specific areas where the above concept applies include the following:

1. Biological macro evolution – Diametrically opposed to biblical creation and real science
2. Relative truth – Diametrically opposed to absolute truth and reality
3. Goodness and perfectibility of man – Diametrically opposed to the biblical declarations and real world observations
4. Man caused global warming – Diametrically opposed to biblical teaching and non-political science
5. Separation of church and state – Diametrically opposed to biblical teaching, its historical origin and the Constitution.
6. Marxism – Diametrically opposed to God, capitalism and biblical principles
7. Freudianism – Goal was to demolish (Christian) religion with psychoanalytic weapons
8. Keynesianism – Diametrically opposed to God, capitalism and Austrian economics
9. Sexual liberation – Part of Communist Manifesto which is diametrically opposed to God and biblical principles
10. Social justice – Code phrase for socialism which is diametrically opposed to capitalism and biblical principles. This is actually a "nice-sounding" euphemism for evil.

It is a fair question to ask why people would want to live inside a dark camera box where their reality is an inverted, false image of the real world rather than living in the real world. The bible answers that question in John 3:19-21 which states:

> [19]And this is the condemnation, that the light has come into the world, and men loved darkness rather than light, because their deeds were evil. [20]For everyone practicing evil hates the light and does not come to the light, lest his deeds should be exposed.

> [21]But he who does the truth comes to the light, that his deeds may be clearly seen, that they have been done in God."

The whole move toward living in the dark camera box and accepting the false inverted image rather than reality has paralleled the rejection of God and the principles of bible truth on a time continuum. Whether one believes in God and the bible or not, the contemporaneous relationship between rejecting both God and biblical truth and cultural degradation is supported. Romans 1:18 explains why those of us that love evil more than truth want to suppress the truth by believing in the inverted false images identified above rather than the truth as follows:

> [18]For the wrath of God is revealed from heaven against all ungodliness and unrighteousness of men, who suppress the truth in unrighteousness,

The bible also addresses those that transpose the true actual image with the diametric opposite. Isaiah 5:20-21 states:

> [20]Woe to those who call evil good, and good evil;
> Who put darkness for light, and light for darkness;
> Who put bitter for sweet, and sweet for bitter!
>
> [21]Woe to those who are wise in their own eyes,
> And prudent in their own sight!

In addition, the bible links those people with loving death. Proverbs 8:36 states:

> [36]But he who sins against me wrongs his own soul;
> All those who hate me love death."

The above concepts are just a start of evidence explaining the existence of God and biblical truth and the existence and effects of diametrically opposite beliefs on our world. The biblical explanations and connections between good and evil appear to match up perfectly with or are a perfect theoretical model for the way our world is. This topic is covered extensively in the book, "Understanding the Anatomy of Evil."

The next chapter will cover the question, "How can Americans be brought back to reality?"

Chapter 9
How Can Americans be Brought Back to Reality?

To reverse the replacement of America's Christian worldview with a godless secular worldview that has happened over the last 50-60 years is a very difficult thing to do. We have been indoctrinating our children with these unbiblical, godless, hedonistic, narcissistic, self-serving, self-destructive beliefs that have destroyed families and made our society sick and corrupt. This has been done in our schools, media, government and even in our churches. Many writers have documented that a very high percentage of our young people have lost their Christian faith and values before finishing their education. Any change agent knows that if you want to change the beliefs within a population you need to start with young people. It is obvious that in any country the beliefs that the young people are taught, whether religious or political, stay firmly established within that population. One analogy would be the ease which a roll of paper towels can be made wet and how difficult it is to dry out the roll. An even better analogy would be getting the roll of paper towels wet with dirty water. That makes the reversal almost impossible.

Any reversal of our dire situation would have to start with a strong leader that has a legitimate platform and a "bully pulpit" that can articulate and expose all the wrong beliefs we have embraced and the disastrous consequences that have resulted from embracing those false beliefs. Some of these concerns with false beliefs include:

- Accepted false foundational beliefs
- Believing stealth evils that are believed to be good

- Legitimizing sexual perversions
- Elevating sensual and destructive pleasures
  - Unbiblical sex
  - Drugs
  - Porn
- Blaming others for our failures
- Allowing evil spirits to control us
- Identifying with churches that compromise biblical doctrine

Most of these are explained in the book "Understanding the Anatomy of Evil."

We need a leader to address all parts of society including academia, media, entertainment and our churches. A cause and effect case needs to be made that links our false beliefs with our downfall. This needs to include both our temporal and future spiritual destiny.

Until we can identify where we have gone wrong and that we are worshiping false gods, no reversal back to where we came from is possible. This reversal will be met with extreme resistance from secularists that love their debauchery and worship the god of this world that is in rebellion against the true God. Just like today, every time a truth is put forth, a plethora of apologists defend the evil belief. We do not want to censure their false belief positions since censorship is evil, but we want to overwhelm them with the light of truth and sheer volume of facts including the first and last word. All false beliefs including political, cultural, philosophical and religious beliefs must be challenged by political, cultural and religious leaders immediately and loudly. All organizations that neglect to do this should be labeled heretical because they are diametrically opposed to biblical principles and consequently are promoting a religion with catastrophic effects in our current world and in the world to come. Today one example of a stealth evil and a false foundational belief that is not countered in any way by our political, cultural or religious leaders is the current "separation of church and state" belief where the Christian religion is treated like a poison. It is amazing, since this belief has no support in our Constitution or in any historical context whether American or European, yet it is accepted without resistance even by our religious leaders. We need a full court press with apologists supporting biblical principles similar to what secularists have done against biblical principles and values.

One huge resistance to any change toward self-reliance is our addiction to positive rights. This includes all the many forms of government financial assistance as well as making us special people and groups. The most recent positive right is the subsidized Affordable Care Act. This not only gives you free money, but it gives you a much higher level of care than you deserve. If you have a preexisting condition it is no longer your problem. Someone else becomes responsible for that. If you have a son in his twenties he is covered under your policy, you no longer have to worry about that. If your lifestyle results in the need for an abortion, it is not your problem. Someone else will pay for that. Need a sex change, no worries. Someone else will pay for it.

This addiction to positive rights bestowed by government is no different than an addiction to alcohol or drugs where tremendous incentive exists to maintain their lifestyle. An alternative analogy is a spoiled child who will throw a huge tantrum if they don't get their way. Thanks to my wife Diane, I just watched "The Miracle Worker" about the early life of Helen Keller. Her parents were so compassionate toward her handicapped condition that they let her have her way on everything. Rather than teaching her discipline and the tools she needed to overcome her handicap, they just pacified her so she wouldn't throw a tantrum. It took an outside, objective person to give her the discipline and knowledge she needed.

With all the demonstrations against Trump we see this exact type of thing. The demonstrators are throwing a tantrum to get their way and maintain their self-serving addictions to government bestowed positive rights and blessings of legitimacy for their illegitimate cause.

Probably one of the biggest concerns dividing our country is racism between the black and white communities. Until we can resolve this issue it is difficult to unify our country to accept biblical truth. We need to identify what is true and what is myth in this realm. To do this we need to only allow historical and statistical facts and disallow emotion to act as a smokescreen to discredit the facts. One emotional area that may feel very real to black people is what is called "white privilege." It means that white people are believed to discriminate against black people without them doing anything discriminatory. That is one emotional area that should not be held against white people. We need to only highlight real discriminations.

In the next chapter we will discuss the evidence explaining the existence of God and biblical truth.

Chapter 10
Evidence Explaining the Existence of God and Biblical Truth

However, for those that do not believe in God and the bible and reject its principles and its truth, much additional evidence exists that supports the existence of God and the truth of the bible. There is also evidence that indicates following its principles results in a safe environment and a contented culture. Alternatively, evidence shows that a culture which rejects God and bible truth and basically lives within a camera box includes high levels of all manner of evil as evidenced in our daily newspapers. David Reagan and Nathan Jones provided the following evidences supporting the existence of God from the Lamb & Lion website. They prefaced their evidence with this statement:

> You probably hear all the time Atheists boldly proclaiming, "There is no God!" They'll mock that if there's an all–powerful, all–knowing, and omnipresent being wouldn't He have left some sort of proof of His existence? They chide that since there's no supposed proof so the ignorant, in order to believe that there is a God, must take some giant leap of faith. "No way there's evidence," they conclude, "so why waste your time?"
>
> Are these skeptics right, or is there proof that God exists?
>
> They're most definitely wrong! I'm going to give you eight proofs that God exists, saving the best for last.[15]

The article continues with eight categories of evidence that God exists as follows:

---
[15] http://christinprophecy.org/?sermons=the-inbox-6-is-there-proof-that-god-exists

#1 — General Revelation, the Teleological Argument

There's an obvious, purposeful design to the universe. With each new scientific discovery—from the atom, to DNA, to our genes, to the cell, and the human eye—Mankind stands amazed at the design, sequencing, and sheer beauty of an incredibly, irreducibly complex world that functions perfectly from the tiniest atom all the way up to the largest galaxy. Within each complexity of design with all the billions of intricate parts working so harmoniously together reveals there has to be a Designer.

The Bible states there's proof of God because there's a creation. "The heavens declare the glory of God; and the firmament shows His handiwork" (Psalm 19:1). The Bible even goes so far as claiming point blank, "He who built all things is God" (Hebrews 3:4).

Whoa, whoa! Wait a moment. The Atheists are accusing that we can't use the Bible to prove God? Okay, not a problem. Then let's look at…

#2 — The Law of Cause and Effect, the Cosmological Argument

Every effect must have an initial cause. Everything that ever came about that began to exist, continues to exist, and stops existing, had a cause. The fact that the universe even exists means there must have been an ultimate, first, uncaused cause—i.e. God.

#3 — The Greatest of the Great, the Ontological Argument

As a kid your parents probably told you, "There will always be someone better than you at…" Whatever you did. There's always someone faster, stronger and smarter. That is, until there is not. You've reached the fastest, strongest, smartest being out there. The greatest possible being must exist, and He is God.

#4 — Life from Life, the Biogenesis Argument

A battery is full of metals and acid and even electricity, but given millions of years, it'll never mutate evolving into a living creature. Life cannot come from non–life. Life only comes from life.

The source of all life is God. Genesis tells us that, "And the Lord God formed man of the dust of the ground, and breathed into his nostrils the breath of life; and man became a living being" (Genesis 2:7).

#5 — The Puzzle that Is Man, the Anthropic Principle

Have you ever pondered over how the conditions on earth have to be perfect in order for life to exist? If the earth wasn't an average of 93 million miles from the sun, we'd bake or freeze. The atmosphere has to have just the right levels of oxygen. Water has to be in abundance. Food has to be readily available. All these countless parameters have to be available and in balance or life wouldn't exist.

And have you noticed that all life on earth can get along just fine without Mankind, but take away any of the other lifeforms and the ecology starts collapsing? It's as if the Earth was designed for the sustaining of people.

And what a world of difference between people and the next closest intelligent creature! We are incredibly more advanced than anything else in nature.

That we can even ponder the question "Why?" shows how different Mankind is from other creatures. We reason, build, love, record history, and stand in awe of beauty—acts that the rest of nature are incapable of performing.

#6 — Conscience, the Moral Argument

Every human being has an innate sense of moral obligation, despite what society they hail from, natural causes, or social factors. We all agree it's wrong to punch a baby, steal money from our neighbor, and cheat to get ahead. Those that disagree, just punch their baby, steal their money, or take an unfair advantage over them and see what they say.

Where did our sense of what is right and wrong come from? If it's genetic, who then wrote morality into our genes?

And how do we identify evil? For there to be evil, then there must be good. How do we know the difference? Romans 2 says it's because we have the law of God written in our hearts, i.e. a conscience.

#7 — Special Revelation, the Religious Experience

While the Atheists certainly haven't met God, sadly, there sure have been a whole lot of other people throughout history who have. God's made quite a number of specific and clear ways of speaking to people, such as through His mighty deeds in history, performing miracles, sending messages through the prophets and apostles, and even coming as a man in the form of His Son, Jesus Christ, all whose writings are found in the Bible (Hebrews 1:1-2).

#8 — The Nation of Israel, the Prophetic Argument

Okay, the best for last, the most irrefutable proof that there is a God can be summed up in one word—Israel.

Go back 3,400 years! Moses reminds the Israelites that they were the only nation God ever took out from the midst of another nation—Egypt—using terrible plagues, and signs and wonders. God did this to prove to His people that the Lord Himself is God, and there is none other besides Him (Deuteronomy 4:25-40).

But this wouldn't be the only time God rescued the Jewish people out from other nations. Moses' last message to the people was a prophecy, a message from God. Moses warned that if they rebelled and broke their covenant with God, He would disperse them to the four corners of the earth and leave the land desolate. But, because of God's great love, He would not abandon them, and in the last days a remnant would be regathered from the nations to return to the newly restored land of Israel (Deuteronomy 28-31).

When this happened, the world would know that God has proven His existence.

History confirms all of this happened just as Moses foretold. The Jews were dispersed—twice!—into the uttermost parts of the earth. But, in just one day—May 14, 1948—the Jewish people became a nation once more after their country was destroyed nearly 1,900 years ago! The dead language of Hebrew was resurrected as the national language. The borders are restored. The strength is there, the bounty is there, and the power is there.

Fulfilled Bible prophecy is the ultimate proof that God exists.

God exists! You're not a piece of space dust evolved over billions of accidents, but a specially created being, and you are loved by your Creator.[16]

Let's add to this evidence for the existence of God that is just a small portion of the evidence documented in the last chapter of "Understanding the Anatomy of Evil." This portion documents Messianic prophecies that support biblical truth.

Messianic Prophecies

Dr. David Reagan of Lamb and Lion Ministries has written a "Christ in Prophecy" study guide[17] that chronicles all the Messianic prophecies as well as other prophecies. Dr. Reagan states that the Bible has about 330 Messianic prophecies of which 108 of them are unique and every one of them fulfilled exactly as predicted. He tells how Dr. Peter Stoner has taken just 8 of the 108 fulfilled Messianic prophecies and calculated the probability of occurring in one individual. The chance of that happening by random chance is one chance in 10 to the 17th power.[18]

Dr. Stoner gave an example that shows us of how small a chance that is. If Texas were covered with silver dollars two feet deep and one marked dollar was randomly placed, a blindfolded person would have to pick would have to the marked dollar on the first try.

That is only for 8 of the 108 prophecies being fulfilled. The chance of all of them being fulfilled like Jesus Christ fulfilled them is impossible on a chance basis. That is the point. Jesus was exactly who the Bible said he was. He was the Son of God incarnated into a man.

Many critics claim that prophecies had to have been written after the events took place because they deny the possibility of the supernatural.

However, scholars agree that all of the Old Testament books were written before Christ. Ra McLaughlin states the following in an

---

[16] http://christinprophecy.org/?sermons=the-inbox-6-is-there-proof-that-god-exists
[17] Dr. David Reagan, Christ in Prophecy Study Guide, (McKinney, TX: Lamb and Lion Ministries, 200X).
[18] Peter W. Stoner, Science Speaks. (Chicago: Moody Press, 1963), p. 100-107.

article titled "Old Testament Dates of Composition in answer to a question of "When was the Old Testament written?":

> The Old Testament was written over a long period of time, ranging from approximately the 15th century B.C. for some of the older books (e.g. Genesis, Exodus) to perhaps as late as the 4th century B.C. for the final forms of some of the most recent books (e.g. Ezra, Nehemiah, Chronicles). Because the Bible itself does not date its books, these dates are the results of scholarly dialogues and conclusions. The date range I have provided includes the most extreme (earliest and latest) dates generally attested by conservative scholars. Liberal scholars tend to set much later dates for many books (into the 2nd century B.C. for some). It is also likely that even the oldest books relied to some degree on prior written sources which have not been preserved through the ages.[19]

In the case of the birth, life, crucifixion and resurrection of Jesus many critics claim that Jesus knew of the prophecies and fulfilled them on purpose. That explanation is completely wishful thinking because Jesus could not have made many of them come true even if he wanted to.

How could he control the following Old Testament prophecies?

Prophecy	O.T. Prophecy Reference	N.T. Prophecy Fulfillment
Virgin conception	Isaiah 7:14	Matthew 1:22-23
Born in Bethlehem	Micah 5:2	Luke 2:4-11
Descendant of Abraham	Genesis 12:1-3	Matthew 1:1
Jewish rejection	Psalms 118:22	I Peter 2:7
Miracles	Isaiah 35:5-6	Matthew 9:35
Ascension	Psalms 68:18	Acts 1:9
Betrayed: 30 pieces of silver	Zechariah 11:12-13	Matthew 27:9-10

---

[19] Ra McLaughlin, Third Millennium, Old Testament of Composition, http://www.thirdmill.org/answers/answer.asp/file/99963.qna/category/ot/page/questions/site/iiim, September 9, 2008.

Prophecy	O.T. Prophecy Reference	N.T. Prophecy Fulfillment
Crucified with thieves	Isaiah 53:12	Luke 23:33
Side would be pierced	Zechariah 12:10	John 19:34
Buried in rich man's tomb	Isaiah 53:9	Matthew 27:57-60
Lots cast for His garments	Psalms 22:18	John 19:23-24
Hands and feet pierced	Psalms 22:16	Luke 23:33
Betrayal money returned	Zechariah 11:13	Matthew 27:3-10
Gall and vinegar offered	Psalms 69:21	Matthew 27:34
No bones broken	Psalms 34:20	John 19:33-36
Daytime darkness at noon	Amos 8:9	Matthew 27:45
Betrayal money: bought field	Zechariah 11:13	Matthew 27:7
Scourged and spit upon	Isaiah 50:6	Mark 14:65
Resurrection	Psalms 16:8-10; 30:3	Luke 24:6, 31-34

This short list includes just 19 prophecies of the unique 108 that exist. Jesus had no control over any of these prophecies. The assertion of skeptics that Jesus simply made sure all the prophecies came true is impossible. The high specificity of the prophecies should be noted. These are not the vague type of prophecies like Nostradamus made. Each one can be and were readily validated. Also, it is interesting and revealing that each of the Old Testament prophecies has a text in the New Testament that verifies the fulfillment. It is also interesting that some of the prophecies from a natural standpoint had virtually no chance of being fulfilled. Crucifixion wasn't even used by the Romans as a form of execution until more than 700 years after the prediction. Who would predict a virgin birth or a resurrection from the dead!

The messianic prophecies alone should convince us that God exists, the supernatural exists and should give us great assurance that the Bible is true and reliable.[20]

Let's add just one more example of a profound, rational, scientific method that proves that good and evil or a legitimate authority exists as well as another illegitimate authority rebelling against it. This complete story is documented in "Understanding the Anatomy of Evil," but we just cover a short synopses here.

This rationale was developed based upon applying probability science to the conclusions documented by Dr. Wayne Grudem in his scholarly 600 page book titled "Politics: According to the Bible." He exhaustively documented 60 plus current two sided political issues and showed that the positions taken by Liberal Progressives are wrong on every one either based upon biblical principles or on facts we know to be true. We showed that the probably of this happening by chance alone without a causal agent is one in a quintillion.

We revealed the significance of being wrong on everything using the following analogy. We asked the reader to pretend that they were a teacher that gave their students a 50 question true / false test with one student getting every question wrong. If we assume that the student didn't have any knowledge of the subject he would typically get about half wrong. The random chance of the student getting 50 incorrect answers is one in a quadrillion.

There are only two possible explanations. One is that he knew all the correct answers, but chose to identify the wrong ones. The only other possibility is that he had a mentor that was in rebellion against the truth or for whatever reason trained his student to support the diametric opposite to the truth! That is exactly what the bible teaches about Satan. He is in rebellion against God, the legitimate authority,

---

[20] William Nitardy, "Understanding the Anatomy of Evil," p. 286-288.

and consequently is diametrically against every truth that God represents. That is a powerful testimony to the existence of God and of biblical truth!

In Chapter 8 we have presented an analogy between two inverted or diametrically opposite images or views of our world. I believe one is the true actual reality that exists and the other is the inverted image in every respect that is diametrically opposite from the real image. We have shown how biblical concepts explain how and why people would actually believe the diametric opposite of the true reality. We have explained that it really doesn't matter if the reader accepts the existence of God and the truth of the bible or rejects those beliefs the contemporaneous timeline between rejecting God and the degradation of our society confirms the relationship. We also showed how both fulfilled biblical prophecy and probability science are very strong evidence of God's existence and the truth of the bible.

Next we will cover Islamic ideology and how it relates to anarchy in America.

Chapter 11
Islamic Ideology

Is Islam a religion or an ideology? I believe that it is both. I don't believe it is too strong to state that it is a totalitarian ideology masquerading as a religion. Let's start by examining the religious roots and attributes of Christianity and Islam and then examine them as ideologies.

History and Attributes of the Christian God

The Christian God is a triune God and is eternal and is the creator of all things and has a character that appears to be perfect and difficult to criticize. Some of these attributes include: wisdom, holiness, omniscience, faithfulness, love, omnipotence, justice, goodness, graciousness and impartiality. Any criticism of Him would likely be about His expectations and judgment that hold us accountable. Historically, the Christian God was involved in His creation with accounts that go as far back as recorded history. He did things like curse His perfect creation after man defiled it, destroyed most of the humans and animals He created. He reprogrammed people's languages to spread them out and prevent them from living in one concentrated urban area. He chose a specific family to represent Him, preserved His Holy writings and provided the way to bring one member of the Godhead to earth as a baby to redeem mankind that had their bloodline infected with sin. That baby was the Messiah, the most prominent figure in history, and Christianity formed as a result of his life, death, resurrection and ascension into heaven. Christianity is still here as a testimony to Jesus the Christ. In addition, the descendants of His chosen people, the Jews, still exist as a people and a country even after being scattered all over the world for almost two thousand years and even speak their revived ancient Hebrew language. For a fantastic presentation of this truth by Dr. David Reagan in a Christ in Prophecy TV program go to the following link: http://christinprophecy.org/?sermons=the-preservation-of-the-jews

Jesus promised to return to the earth in like manner as He ascended into heaven. About this same time, the bible teaches that an anti-Christ will arise and become a one-world leader along with a false prophet promoting a one-world religion and will kill Christians and Jews. Keep this in mind so it can be compared with Islamic teaching.

History and Attributes of the Islamic God

Allah is both the name of the Islamic god as well as the generic name for god in Arabic. Although the religion of Islam originated about 600 AD with Muhammad, their specific god, Allah, didn't originate with Islam and wasn't the Jewish and Christian God Jehovah. The following quotes support this assertion:

> Interestingly, not many Muslims want to accept that Allah was already being worshipped at the Ka'ba in Mecca by Arab pagans before Muhammad came. Some Muslims become angry when they are confronted with this fact. But history is not on their side. Pre-Islamic literature has proved this." (Who is this Allah?, G. J. O. Moshay, 1994, p 138)

> "But history establishes beyond the shadow of doubt that even the pagan Arabs, before Muhammad's time, knew their chief god by the name of Allah and even, in a sense, proclaimed his unity...Among the pagan Arabs this term denoted the chief god of their pantheon, the Kaaba, with its three hundred and sixty idols." (The Moslem Doctrine of God, Samuel M. Zwemer 1905, p 24-25)[21]

Another quote stated the following:

---

[21] http://www.bible.ca/islam/islam-allah-pre-islamic-origin.htm

"Before Muhammad appeared, the Kaaba was surrounded by 360 idols, and every Arab house had its god. Arabs also believed in jinn (subtle beings), and some vague divinity with many offspring. Among the major deities of the pre-Islamic era were *al-Lat* ("the Goddess"), worshipped in the shape of a square stone; *al-Uzzah* ("the Mighty"), a goddess identified with the morning star and worshipped as a thigh-bone-shaped slab of granite between al-Taid and Mecca; Manat, the goddess of destiny, worshipped as a black stone on the road between Mecca and Medina; and the moon god, Hubal, whose worship was connected with the Black Stone of Kaaba.

The stones were said to have fallen from the sun, moon, stars, and planets and to represent cosmic forces. The so-called Black Stone (actually the color of burnt amber) that Muslims revere today is the same one that their forebears had worshipped well before Muhammad and that they believed had come from the moon."[22]

In addition to the Islamic god Allah being associated with the Pagan idol gods the following quote identifies Allah and the symbol of Islam, the crescent moon, as associated with Satan and Ba'al:

In Judges 8:21, the word used for crescent is saharon, which literally means 'crescent moon'. It comes from the root word sahar, which is literally used for the name of Satan in Isaiah 14 as Hilal ben Sahar. Hilal, or heylal, is the word that the King James Bible translates as Lucifer. The full phrase actually means "morning star/ crescent moon," which is the very symbol of Islam. In other words, the symbol of Islam and the name of Satan are one and the same. This is significant and a very clear hint into the spiritual origins of Islam and the Antichrist.

So we see that the ancient enemies of Israel worshiped a God that was symbolized by the image of the crescent moon. To this day, this has not changed. In fact, all evidence points to the fact that Allah is simply another name for Bel or Baal, which simply means "lord" and is also the title of reverence to the Babylonian moon-god. The Romans had the same god, and so did the Greeks, who worshiped the Gog (Gygez), a war deity called Men. This is also the god that Abraham left behind for Jehovah, the one true God. It comes as no surprise then that Jesus referred to Satan as Beelzebub (Ball Thubab, Arabic) (Matthew 12:24-27). The Hastings Encyclopedia of Religion

---

[22] http://www.adishakti.org/_/before_muhammad_appeared_the_kaaba.htm

and Ethics confirms the fact that the Arab name "Allah" correlates to Bel: "Allah is a pre-Islamic name…corresponding to the Babylonian god known as Bel."[23]

Allah is not a personal god with loving attributes like Jehovah, the Christian God. The Qur'an itself states that Allah is the great deceiver, the diametric opposite of Jehovah. The following verses from the Qur'an state:

> And they deceived, and Allah deceived. And Allah is the best deceiver.[24]

> And they deceived and Allah deceived. And Allah is the best deceiver.[25]

> Will he whose evil deed is adorned to him so he sees it as good? So surely Allah leads astray whom he wills.[26]

Consequently, it is obvious from the Qur'an that Allah is Satan, the deceiver that is against Jehovah the Christian God and us. This is confirmed by the exacting similarities between the Islamic savior, the Mahdi, and the Christian anti-Christ. The following list from "Understanding the Anatomy of Evil" includes 40 plus similar attributes that verify the similarity of the Christian anti-Christ and the Islamic savior, the Mahdi:[27]

- Both deny the trinity and the cross
- Both deny the Father and the Son
- Both are Blasphemous
- Both are called deceiver
- Both attempt to deceive Christians and Jews
- Both practice deception through Kitman and Taqiyya
- Both claim to be Messiah
- Both kingdoms suffer a head wound
- Both work false miracles
- Both ride a white horse
- Both attempt to change the law

---

[23] Walid Shoebat and Joel Richardson, "God's War on Terror," 2nd Addition, 2010, p. 384-385.
[24] Usama K. Dakdok, "The Generous Qur'an," Usama Dakdok Publishing, LLC, Venice, FL, Sura 3:54, p. 35.
[25] Ibid., Sura 8:30, p. 107.
[26] Ibid., Sura 35:8, p. 251.
[27] William Nitardy, "Understanding the Anatomy of Evil," p. 75-76.

- Both deny women's rights
- Both rule over ten entities
- Both are source of death and war
- Both use military force
- Both honor their god with Gold and Silver
- Both honor a god of war and advance his glory through war
- Both condone rape
- Both usher in a seven year peace treaty
- Both deceive and destroy by peace
- Both break treaties
- Both love war for booty
- Both desire world domination
- Both lead a Turkish-Iranian invasion
- Both exalted as god
- Both ascend to heaven
- Both are described as a Beautiful and wise bird
- Both are beings of light
- Both are pride-filled
- Both are lords of this world and the underworld
- Both are called the "Son of the dawn"
- Both are afflicters
- Both are cast out of heaven
- Both are the lord of demons
- Both are possessed
- Both practice beheading
- Both desire Israel's destruction
- Both occupy the temple mount
- Our Messiah is their Antichrist and their Antichrist is our Messiah
- Both stop the rain
- Both enjoy desecrating bodies

For 40 plus attributes above, the chances of all the Christian anti-Christ's characteristics being the same as all the Islamic savior's characteristics by random chance is 2^{40} or one chance in a trillion. Consequently, it is no coincidence and proves that their savior is our anti-Christ.

Opposite Idealogies / Opposite Results

When we have a creator God that has all the desirable characteristics that are listed at the beginning of this chapter, and an adversarial god or powerful being in rebellion against the true God, wouldn't we expect a hating, destructive power rather that a loving, supportive father figure?

It is amazing that in our world all of this mostly obvious factual information on Islam is so successfully suppressed. Both religious skeptics and prominent Christian leaders including the pope and our last two presidents have stated that the Islamic god and the Christian God are the same god. We have numerous apologists assuring us that all the so-called terrorism carried out by Muslims is not related or associated to the Islamic religion. Although all the terrorists are Muslims, they never associate the source of the terrorism as Islamic ideology. We have former president Obama stating the Islamic State is not Islamic. The Obama administration declared the Nidal Hasan attack on Fort Hood as workplace violence rather than Islamic terrorism. The evidence could not have been more obvious including his background and yelling Allahu Akbar while killing the solders. We have had the rules rewritten for the FBI so Islam is never implicated when all the Muslims are terrorizing us. This is insane!

With very little study of the Qur'an both the motivation to kill or subjugate non-Muslims and the methods of torture, murder and deception are clearly obvious. Terrorism is strictly a strategy for conquering and controlling. It is not an ideology that supplies a motivation to carry out the terror and killing. Not only do we never identify the motivating ideology of the terrorists we go to extreme lengths to prevent linking any terrorism to Islamic ideology.

The only possible explanation must be that we have been infiltrated with Muslims and Islamic sympathizers. What else could explain the suppression of the truth but an endless stream of apologists?

The next chapter connects Islam with the anarchy infested demonstrations occurring after Trump's inauguration.

Chapter 12
Relating Islam to American Anarchy

Now that President Trump has been sworn in as our 45th president, anarchists are raising havoc across the country through protests and demonstrations. One such type of protests is organized women's marches. Below is a great article by Garth Kant with the perspective of Cheri Berens.

Berens is an American who has lived in Cairo for years working as a researcher for the Egyptian Ministry of Culture. She witnessed the violence that preceded the takeover of the country by the radical Muslim Brotherhood and the counter-revolution that removed it from power.

Women's March protesters in Washington on Jan. 21.

WASHINGTON – They gathered by the thousands to watch history on television.

They cheered wildly when President Trump said in his inaugural address that the U.S. will eradicate radical Islamic terrorism from the face of the earth. The next day, they looked on in shock and horror at the violent protests in the streets. They were even more horrified when they saw American women wearing hijabs, Muslim headscarves worn as a sign of piety.

But this wasn't Kansas. It wasn't even the Midwest. It was the Middle East. Cairo, Egypt. Home to tens of millions of devout Muslims. Cheri Berens saw it first-hand. From her vantage point, "The entire coffee shop gasped in disbelief at the vision of American women donning the headscarf."

Berens is an American who has lived in Cairo for years working as a researcher for the Egyptian Ministry of Culture. She witnessed the violence that preceded the takeover of the country by the radical Muslim Brotherhood and the counter-revolution that removed it from power. Berens is author of "Cheri's Memoir: An American Woman Living in Egypt" and is working on her next book, "The Cultural History of Egypt." And, in an essay on her blog titled "Women's March to Islam?" she chronicled how for everyday Egyptians watching on television, packed into "every coffee shop in Cairo that had a satellite dish," the scenes in the streets of Washington, D.C., were disturbingly familiar.

They recognized the same methods the Muslim Brotherhood used for decades to finally seize control in Egypt playing out in the American capital. "First we saw protesters smashing windows and torching cars," wrote Berens. "Hushed murmuring began around me as every single Egyptian in the coffee shop could be heard saying the words: 'Muslim Brotherhood.'"

She observed: "The images we were watching could have been taken right from a street in Egypt. It is exactly what we had experienced on a daily basis for more than a year." While the violence stunned the Egyptians, it was American women wearing hijabs that evoked agitation and even anger.

We have been fighting to remove the headscarf. Why are these the stupid women putting them on?" asked an Egyptian woman within earshot of Berens. Indeed, it is a question many have asked: Why would American women, and even the homosexual community, make common cause with those who would strip them of their rights and civil liberties?

WND put that question to former U.S. Rep. Michele Bachmann, R-Minn., who once introduced legislation to designate the Muslim Brotherhood as a terrorist organization and who observed that the question of why collaboration occurs among disparate causes comes up often.

"People understand Islam abhors homosexuality, yet they often join forces in protests with gay activists," she told WND. "The answer is simple, Black Lives Matters, the gay agenda, as well as Islamic supremacism, all seek domination over American freedoms."

Still, why collaborate? "They cannot reach their aims separately, but they can realize the fall of individual liberties if they work together. Once liberties fall, the groups break with each other in a race to impose their particular views on the American populace," Bachmann explained. "Causing liberties to fall is a long-term project, and they will use whatever allies they can get to realize that phase of their goals," she concluded.

That strategy seemed apparent in what Berens observed. Berens remarked how no one would ever think of damaging someone's car or business before 2012, the year the Muslim Brotherhood took power in Egypt. But after that, "mobs of Muslim brotherhood would 'protest' in the streets, ripping apart public and private property and disabling normal activity—just as we were now watching on TV." "Some of the 'protesters' even covered their faces in the exact same way the Muslim brotherhood do."

Kant continues:

Making Egyptians even more uneasy was seeing police reduced to what Berens called a quasi-helpless state. "Again the words 'Muslim Brotherhood' were mumbled throughout the coffee shop. The Muslim Brotherhood had disabled our police force via accusations of police brutality long before the violent protest began."

She explained: "Via a well-calculated program of propaganda and lies, they were able to make the police force impotent. Police became afraid to stop the protest for fear of being accused brutality." Egyptians have experienced their own version of what's come to be called the "Ferguson effect" and the epidemic of police shootings last summer in the wake of the Black Lives Matter protests.

"During the last two weeks, 29 police officers have been killed in Egypt," observed Berens. "Once the Muslim Brotherhood put this idea of 'police brutality' into place, police officers became fair game and are killed on a regular basis. Before 2012, killing a police officer was absolutely unheard of."

Berens detected Muslim Brotherhood influence among the Washington protesters and rioters, and one facet may help explain how something many Egyptians consider a sign of oppression, the hijab, became a trendy accessory for some American women during their march.

One of the four main organizers of Saturday's Women's March was Linda Sarsour, a pro-Palestine Muslim activist who supports Shariah law, the strict Islamic code that renders women thoroughly subservient to men. Sarsour worked with the Obama administration as to what they called a "Champion of Change" and was a delegate to the Democratic National Convention. She also is affiliated with the Council on American-Islamic Relations, an un-indicted co-conspirator in the Holy Land Foundation terrorism financing case. Sarsour was seen recently posing for photos at a Muslim convention in Chicago with an accused financier for the Palestinian terrorist group Hamas.

Get the WND Books bestseller "See Something, Say Nothing" by former DHS agent Philip Haney to learn how he exposed the Obama administration's submission to jihad.

Kant continues:

Berens said the Egyptians with whom she watched the protests were bewildered by the explanation offered on television that the women were marching for civil rights. "The women in the coffee shop shook their heads and asked, 'Rights? The headscarf will take away your rights!' one young woman shouted at the TV."

Berens recounted how the grand mufti of al-Ahzar, the highest authority in Sunni Islam, has ruled that the headscarf is not a religious requirement. She said that is well known to anyone who has read the Quran or studied Islam. "And here, in front of our eyes, were non-Muslim, American women donning the headscarf!" "In Muslim countries such as Egypt," she continued, "women who do not wear a headscarf are often sexually harassed or attacked. They are beaten; they are raped; and sometimes, they are killed."

"In 2012, when the Muslim Brotherhood took power, there were several attacks on Christian women on trains. They were grabbed, their hair chopped off, they were pushed off fast-moving trains. They were told they must wear headscarf—even though they are not Muslim."

Berens stated plainly, "Any country in which the headscarf is imposed, women always suffer from abuses and restrictions." That included, she said, the law imposed by ISIS in al-Qaida in Syria against women sitting in chairs, because it will stimulate them and make them "go out of control with lust." Out of the same fear, women in certain areas of the Sudan are barred from wearing pants.

"In most Muslim communities," Berens observed, "even Muslim communities in America, the headscarf eventually leads to the full veil, because the headscarf leads to the belief that women easily become sexually 'out of control,' or they become too 'tempting.'"

Berens said that is what American women should be protesting. And she made a bold declaration: "This 'women's march' wasn't about Trump. Trump is being used as a scapegoat for the Muslim agenda."

It was her research that led her to such a stark conclusion. "I follow more than 100 Muslim Brotherhood groups in America and also several of their most powerful activists. They were all promoting this Women's March." She then used a phrase more often associated with the previous president: "The activists, who call themselves 'community organizers,' targeted African-Americans and Hispanics, but even more heavily targeted was the LBGT community, pro-choice groups, and vulnerable university students."

Berens echoed Bachmann's observations about groups that would otherwise seem to be natural enemies coming together for a common cause. She noted that "Muslims despise homosexuals" and that homosexuality is punishable by death in Islam, yet the Muslim organizations promoting the event targeted the LBGT community and claimed to promote their rights.

Kant continues:

> The author said that was done to enlist their aid, as Muslims have done with Christian and Jewish groups in attacking so-called

"Islamophobia." Berens said the Muslims targeted pro-choice American women for the same reason, despite the fact that "abortions are illegal in Islam and no Muslim woman would dare have one." She warned: "They want American women to have abortions. They want the non-Muslim population to be stagnant while their Muslim population grows. Numbers mean power."

Berens also noted that the Muslim Student Association targeted students throughout the United States to go to the march. "They have their finger on the pulse of the 'gender identity crisis.' They want American youth to be confused and frozen. They want American youth to be non-productive beings obsessed with their 'civil right' to a 'safe space' and 'time outs.'" That, she suggested, was the radical Muslims' endgame.

"They want a young male population that is weakened, or with confused female tendencies, whether real, imagined or transgendered. They want to confuse the American youth so they are helpless and unable to fight. They want to oppress the women and weaken the men." And to that end, Berens maintains, subversive Muslims are employing misdirection.

"Most Americans have been focused on the stupidity of some of the goings on at the Women's March instead of the deviousness of it. They want you distracted so that you won't see what is really happening behind the scenes." And who does Berens blame for all the misinformation about the radical Muslims' true intentions? The American media.

She concluded with a revelation and a stark warning. "Very powerful Muslim Brotherhood organizations helped organize and promote this event targeting very specific groups. And, starting in 1962, the Muslim Brotherhood placed very powerful people in the media profession to co-opt the media." And, a footnote, in case one would wonder: Why would Muslims in one of the most Islamic nations in the world erupt in cheers at President Trump's promise to wipe out radical Islamic terrorism?

Berens made an observation that revealed some Americans might have more in common with the average Egyptian than they realize.

"We here in Egypt have experienced many terror attacks and all of us have experienced the death of a friend or family member who were members of the Army and who fight ISIS on a daily basis."[28]

This is a wonderful insight through the eyes of someone who has an international perspective of what is going on in America and how it relates to the Muslim Brotherhood and a stealth destruction of America. We also need to see what is going on with the same perspective if we are going to avoid destruction.

---

[28] http://www.wnd.com/2017/01/why-were-protesters-wearing-hijabs/

Chapter 13
Final Thoughts

With our main focus on the rights vs responsibilities of groups, we have exposed that the groups leading protests demand their rights while rejecting any responsibility for their beliefs or actions. They hide behind a nice sounding euphemism that doesn't represent their mission or goal. This allows them to garner much public support based upon their misleading euphemistic title whereas if they had a representative title or were open about just wanting power for their group their support would be minimal. Solutions were presented to address these deceptions that allow illegitimate organizations an aura of legitimacy.

We also covered the sensitive and confusing facts concerning racism. We showed that any serious white on black racism is virtually non-existent. Alternatively, facts were presented that showed that while black on white racism was rampant, blacks will not give whites credit for the enormous progress that has been made in their favor. We need to separate facts from emotion in the racial area and reject emotional appeals and base all conclusions on facts.

We need to stop basing alleged white on black discrimination upon an expectation of financial equal outcomes. In addition, we need to stop basing alleged discriminatory treatment by police upon assumptions that criminal behavior is the same between blacks and whites. The rejection of "search and frisk" and profiling likely law breakers in high crime areas only legitimatizes black criminals. Whether black, white, Asian or Hispanic the primary financial and law abiding responsibility primarily lies within each group.

We showed how our belief systems in the last 60 years have turned upside down so now we believe just the opposite of what was believed previously. Consequently, now rather than living in the real world of true facts and reality we are living in an opposite virtual reality that is analogous to living inside a camera box where everything is reversed. We explained that contrary to what one would think, that this reversal is actually clearly explained in several biblical texts. We covered what we need to do to bring us back to reality, where we were earlier.

In the author's previous book "Understanding the Anatomy of Evil," an entire part including four chapters used diametric opposition as a scientific method of proving that actual things in politics and religion reveal that "behind the scenes" forces are active rather than things happening by random chance. A taste of that rationale was also covered in this book. We can clearly see the conflict of two polar opposite worldviews in America and around the world today. We have never been more polarized. We believe based upon evidence that this conflict is a spiritual battle between good and evil. The obvious solution, and our choice, is to reject evil and embrace good. However, the polar opposite worldview, which I believe is promoted by the evil side, is perfectly represented by the "coexist" bumper sticker. The typical bumper sticker looks like this:

The actual significance of each letter of symbol is as follows:

Every letter in the "COEXIST" phrase has a symbol representing a religious system or spiritual ideology: "C" for the crescent and star (representing Islam); "O" being dotted with the Karma Wheel (Buddhism) "E" as energy in the relativity equation (Science); "X" illustrating the star of David (Judaism); the "I" representing the pentagram (Wicca/Pagan); "S" for the Tao symbol; and "T" for the cross for Christianity.[29]

However, we need to add some additional significance to several of these letters. The "O" also represents the peace sign with all of its implications. The "e" also represents homosexuality. Some really good comments about this symbol and its significance are as follows:

> The goal of this movement is the promotion of a pluralistic and universal utopian worldview. At the heart of this movement is the abandonment of core absolutes and values for a relativistic delusion (moral and spiritual). This movement seeks to undermine personal beliefs and practices for the supposed "betterment" of world unification. Its most damnable feature, however, is the staunch rejection of the sovereignty and reality of Almighty God, His authoritative Word (the Bible), and His Savior to all fallen men, the Lord Jesus Christ (John 14:6; Acts 4:12; 1 John 2:22-23).[30]

The article continues:

> A phrase from the Coexist website states, *"Coexist is a concept brand for everyone, connecting people and planet, together we symbolize life, love and global harmony."*
>
> The Coexist phenomenon is the product of the subjective secular Left. The majority of the Coexist followers are secular liberals. This ideology of religious pluralism actually intersects with all three political ideologies (liberal, moderate, and conservative), but it has its greatest hold in the secular liberal mind (Romans 1:18-32; 8:5-8).
>
> The true core of the Left are secularists who wish to promote a delusional, pluralistic universe that combines all godless ideologies. However, their main goal and real agenda is to rid the world of all religious ideologies in favor of a secular, godless one.[31]

I would certainly agree with these comments. This is basically the one world religion that the bible describes will be established at the end of the Age. With this religion, truth and facts do not matter, only

---

[29] The "Coexist" Movement and Delusion, http://www.theignorantfishermen.com/2009/08/coexist-movement-and-delusion_24.html
[30] Ibid.
[31] Ibid.

an emotional appeal to get along for the sake of unity. Certainly, Islam does not believe in or teach unity, does not allow religious liberty and its M.O. initially is stealth, but ultimately the use of force. Christianity also does not believe in unity in respect to other religions that are false, but it does believe in religious liberty and its M.O. is not coercive. Consequently, the only way to have the appearance of unity ala "Coexist" is through deception. This is where Lucifer and Allah excel.

What's most important is to have a proper perspective of good and evil through a biblical lens. When we have a conflict of interest that results from our unrighteousness or chemical, physical or mental addictions to worldly idols we cannot objectively judge good vs. evil.

Although not generally recognized, there is an increasing attack on the bible and Christians and Christian values. Kelly Shackelford, the chief counsel for First Liberty, reported the following:

> Hostility to religion in America is rising like floodwaters...This flood is engulfing ordinary citizens who simply try to live normal lives according to their faith and conscience. It is eroding the bedrock on which stand vital American institutions such as government, education, the military, businesses, houses of worship, and charity. It has the potential to wash away the ground that supports our other rights, including freedom of speech, press, assembly and government by consent of the people.[32]

Although it is people that perpetrate all the evils in the world, we need to see people as victims of the false narrative that puts them in bondage to evil and see them as potential converts to the truth. Currently, in America we actually are seeing converts going the other way, from truth to evil. The following quote validates this but also confirms that many Muslims in the Muslim world are converting to Christianity:

> While we see Christianity on the steady decline in America, we see it on the rise in other nations. In June 2015, *Christianity Today* published an article proclaiming, "We are living in the midst of the greatest turning of Muslims to Christ in history."[33]

---

[32] Carl Gallups, "When the Lion Roars," WND Books, Washington D.C., p.264.
[33] Ibid., p. 268.

The same thing is also happening in China with many converting to Christianity.

Albert Einstein stated:

> The world is a dangerous place to live, not because of the people that are evil, but because of the people who don't do anything about it.

Obviously the people who are in the best position to do something about it and also are the ones that we would expect to take a stand against evil are our pastors. They are supposed to be our shepherds of truth and have the natural megaphone at least once a week to speak out and yet they have been strangely silent about our cultural, political, philosophical and religious evils. When nobody speaks against the evil false narratives people naturally accept them as truth. "Understanding the Anatomy of Evil" encouraged pastors to take a worldview quiz to hone their worldview and then to speak out against evil. The back cover of the book asked the question: Are you helping expose evil or are you promoting evil? We are doing one or the other. Until we all join in and do the former, America will continue to slide toward destruction.

www.ingramcontent.com/pod-product-compliance
Lightning Source LLC
Chambersburg PA
CBHW072103290426
44110CB00014B/1810